www.finishinglinepress.com

ALL WE HAVE LOVED

essays by

Julia Nunnally Duncan

Finishing Line Press
Georgetown, Kentucky

ALL WE HAVE LOVED

Publisher: Leah Huete de Maines
Editor: Christen Kincaid
Cover Art: Julia Nunnally Duncan
Author Photo: Steve Duncan
Cover Design: Elizabeth Maines McCleavy

Order online: www.finishinglinepress.com
          also available on amazon.com

Author inquiries and mail orders:
Finishing Line Press
P. O. Box 1626
Georgetown, Kentucky 40324
U. S. A.

Table of Contents

III

*This book is offered in loving memory of my mother,
Madeline Davis Nunnally (1922-2020), whose endearing stories of her
Clinchfield cotton mill village childhood inspired me,
and in loving memory of my brother,
Donald "Butch" Nunnally (1942-2020).*

And the memories of all we have loved stay and come back to us in the evening of our life. They are not dead but sleep, and it is well to gather a treasure of them.

—Vincent van Gogh, *The Letters of Vincent van Gogh*

Introduction

Home is important to me. As I look at my body of creative work, I see common threads—memories of home and people (and animals) that have impacted my life.

My hometown in Western North Carolina is not extraordinary in comparison to other Southern locales. Yet it has been my world. Marion, once a thriving textile town from the early 1900s to the late 20th century, has offered a reasonable livelihood to industrious inhabitants, including my parents, who always worked in hosiery mills. I had the opportunity to visit those mills as a child. One mill in particular was special to us, and our lives were changed by a catastrophe at that mill ("Saturdays at the Mill"). My mother grew up in a cotton mill village, her father having been an overseer in the card room at Clinchfield Manufacturing Company. As noted in "Her Clinchfield Childhood," she witnessed the Marion Textile Strike of 1929, a labor upheaval notorious enough to draw the attention of Woody Guthrie and Sinclair Lewis. In my mother's later years, she enjoyed revisiting her old haunts in the Clinchfield community and, I believe, always considered Clinchfield her home.

My childhood home was in a working-class neighborhood, still rural in those days, located not far from town. Our neighborhood was friendly and filled with adults of all ages, children, dogs, and livestock ("A Horse of My Own"). The neighborhood has changed through the years, as examined in "The Party." Yet this neighborhood and the house I grew up in will always be home to me, though I haven't lived there in decades. This place and my experiences there find their way into many of my works.

My residence now in a western area of McDowell County—the childhood home of my husband, Steve, built on his family's ancestral land—has offered challenges and adventures, attested by "Copperheads," "Hornets' Nest," and "The Christmas Hawk." Our home and the surrounding mountainous terrain are especially dear to Steve, who, like my mother and me, has a keen sense of connection to place ("Those Golden Years" and "The Wampus Kitty").

I have a strong allegiance to family and the past, evidenced by many of my essays, such as "My Mother's Snow Cream," "My Uncle Paul," and "My Father's Pocket Knives." In other essays, including "Her Wedding Ring" and "The Stone Cutter's Tools," the long-dead family members who are central characters are known to me only through oral history and old photographs, but they are kin, nevertheless, and I honor their lives—complex, troubled, heroic, and worthy of remembrance and respect.

I agree with Vincent van Gogh that the memories of all we have loved—a place, family, and lifelong experiences—are never dead. And I, too, believe it is worth our while to gather these memories and treasure them. I hope the reader will find my gathering of such memories enjoyable and compelling.

—Julia Nunnally Duncan

I

Night Visitor

The memory is dream-like now, but some parts are vivid as if the events happened yesterday.

It was a summer evening in the early 1960s. My parents, older brother Steve, and I joined my father's younger sister and her family for an overnight trip to the Great Smoky Mountains. We piled into my uncle's truck, most of us riding in the truck bed, for the two hour drive to East Tennessee from our home in Marion, North Carolina.

My family members were not seasoned campers. Our outdoor adventures had mainly been confined to short hikes in the woods near my grandmother's house and leisurely Sunday afternoon drives on the Blue Ridge Parkway, which was a short distance from our home. So this camping trip to the Smokies was unusual for us.

When we arrived in Tennessee, we didn't seek a campground that offered picnic tables, grills, or bathroom facilities. Instead, we simply pulled off the road onto a grassy shoulder and entered the woods to make our campsite.

We built no campfire to cook hotdogs or toast marshmallows. Rather, we ate the meal my mother and aunt had prepared at home and packed for our supper.

At dusk, while the rest of our group sat around and talked, I tagged along with my father and his brother-in-law as they strolled down a path for their final smoke of the evening. My father was a heavy cigarette smoker then, his pack of Camels always stored in his front shirt pocket.

As darkness fell, we settled down for the night. No tents, air mattresses, or sleeping bags had been brought for our comfort. Our tent was the starry sky and canopy of tree limbs above us; our beds, the patchwork quilts we spread on the forest floor. The mountain air, cool and pungent with the scent of firs and pines, was our coverlet.

Sometime in the night, I was startled from sleep by my mother who was awake and standing beside me.

"What's goin' on?" I asked and stood, unsteady on my bare feet and rubbing my eyes, still half-shut from drowsiness.

"Ssh!" she responded and grasped my shoulder to quieten me and keep me still.

I noticed that others in our group, dazed and groggy, were awake, too. Everyone seemed to be looking at my father, who remained asleep on his quilt.

In the moonlight, we watched as a large black bear slowly circled my father.

The adults kept their children at a safe distance, and we were all hushed with fear, the only sounds being the bear's paws crunching the undergrowth and my father's vigorous snoring. As long as I knew him, my father was a deep sleeper and heavy snorer, and this night was no exception.

While we stood watching—no one shooing the bear, perhaps thinking that our noise would only anger it—the bear stepped onto my father's quilt and sniffed it. Soon, though, it lost interest and ambled off into the darkness, leaving my father unscathed and oblivious to its presence.

The next morning, before we headed back home, we told my father about his night visitor.

"It 'bout stepped on you," I said. "It was big."

"Like Papa Bear?" he asked and smiled. He knew that "Goldilocks and the Three Bears" was my favorite bedtime story—one he had told me many times.

"Yeah," I confirmed.

My father had been a Merchant Marine during World War II, who ferried supplies in a Liberty ship, the *SS Booker T. Washington,* to England, France, and Belgium. During these voyages across the Atlantic, his ship entered the war zone and risked U-boat attacks. And now here in the Smokies he had faced another kind of danger. Yet he didn't seem fazed when we recounted the bear incident. In fact, I'm not sure he even believed us.

But what we told him was true, and I have the memory to prove it.

After that brief but memorable camping experience, my family traveled many weekends to the Smoky Mountains to enjoy the unique culture of the Cherokee Indian Reservation and the colorful shops of Gatlinburg, Tennessee.

During these weekend getaways, however, we spent our nights in a motel.

Baptism

But Jesus said, Suffer little children,
and forbid them not, to come unto me:
for of such is the kingdom of heaven.

King James Version, Matthew 19.14

Though I joined the Episcopal Church when I was nineteen, I was raised in the Southern Baptist Church. So when my Episcopal rector recently referred to his grandmother's having been a "Lottie Moon Southern Baptist," I was taken back to my own childhood.

As a child in the 1960s, I, too, was a Lottie Moon Southern Baptist. On certain mornings as part of the preaching service, one of our members, Jessie Mae, stood before the congregation and gave a plea for the Lottie Moon offering, a mission fund named in honor of a Southern Baptist missionary to China who lived in the nineteenth and early twentieth centuries.

During the 1960s, other concerns were also brought before the congregation. When the Vietnam War escalated and young men from our community went to serve in that war, prayers were offered for "our boys in foreign fields." These long prayers on Sunday were usually led by my uncle Paul in his deep baritone voice. A World War II Army veteran who had himself been severely injured in North Africa, Paul could appreciate the mortal risks the Vietnam soldiers faced. And being a redeemed sinner, whose past days were filled with dissolute behavior and heavy drinking, which he had relinquished through repentance and salvation, he also understood the power of prayer.

Our minister, Reverend Sprinkle, whom we called *Preacher Sprinkle,* was reserved and congenial, but during his sermons, his voice grew intense and his face turned blood red. He preached sin and redemption with fervor reminiscent of Reverend Billy Graham, our Montreat neighbor.

I was a bashful child, and our preacher's sermons put the fear of God in me. But maybe more importantly, his words stirred my soul to acknowledge its guilt. As far as I know, the only sin I had committed in my early days was stealing. Perhaps the preacher quoted the Commandment "Thou shalt not steal," and this struck a nerve. At around four years old, I was visiting my neighbor Marie's house, and her teenage daughter, Kaye, was playing the piano for me. When Kaye finished playing and left the room, I lingered behind and sneaked a miniature horse figurine from the piano's top. Even then, I was a horse lover and apparently couldn't resist the little horse. When I arrived home, my mother noticed that I gripped something in my hand.

"What are you holding?" she asked. And when she saw the figurine, she said, "Where did you get that?"

I whimpered, "Marie's." She could tell from my sheepish manner that Marie had not given me the horse.

"You take that right back," she ordered, "and say you're sorry!"

Crying as I walked across the street and into our neighbor's house, I slipped into the room where the piano sat and placed the figurine where I had found it.

As I came back into Marie's living room, she saw me and noticed my tears. "What's wrong?" she asked.

I couldn't answer for crying and ran out her front door and back across the street. As soon as I walked in our front door, my mother said, "Did you take it back?" I still couldn't talk and just nodded my head, deeply hurt and ashamed.

I never touched the horse figurine again, though Marie probably would have given it to me if she'd known I wanted it.

This theft, which was an aberration in my early character that I still don't understand, left an indelible mark on my conscience. So when Preacher Sprinkle made an altar call one Sunday morning when I was seven, I grew anxious. The choir, led by my uncle Lloyd, compellingly sang "Just As I Am." As I listened, I felt that the words were directed at me. I sat on the hard, polished pew, growing more uneasy by the hymn's haunting refrain "I come! I come!"

"Won't you come forward, my beloved," the preacher coaxed, "and give your heart to Jesus?" He seemed to be speaking to me.

I looked beside me at my mother, stylish and pretty in her pastel dress, and down the pew at my father, strong and broad-shouldered in his suit and tie, and at my eleven-year-old brother Steve in his dress shirt and slacks. I knew I had been called, so I rose from my seat.

As I went forward, I noticed other kids from my Sunday school class standing, too. When we reached the altar, we knelt in a line. The preacher spoke with each of us, reverently questioning and receiving our convictions. He announced what a joy it was that we children had come forward, dedicating our hearts to Jesus. A chorus of "Amens" passed through the large white sanctuary, and I heard my uncle Paul's voice rise above them all.

Our baptism was scheduled for an upcoming Sunday to be held in the church's baptistery, which was located in a curtained alcove behind the choir section.

On the day of my baptism, the baptismal pool had been filled and the dark curtain opened. I was excited, but a little afraid of getting strangled during the immersion. I had seen this happen when others had been baptized in our church. When my mother, father, and Steve were baptized the year before, my mother had been apprehensive about getting water in her nose or mouth. She had never learned to swim, so she felt vulnerable facing a total immersion. My father had already taught me how to dogpaddle and float, and I knew how to hold my breath when my head went under water. The mountain stream where he taught me to swim was located a few miles west of my home and was a favorite swimming hole for kids in our community. On summer days, my father took Steve and me and any neighborhood kids who could fit in our car for a swim. He carried along a bar of Zest soap, and while we swam, he stood downstream and lathered his bare chest and arms.

Occasionally when we first arrived for our swim, eager to scurry down the woodsy bank to the water, we noticed a group of people in Sunday clothes standing down at the water's edge, gathered for a baptism. My father made us wait quietly until the baptism was over.

A baptism was a holy sacrament not to be taken lightly, and witnessing another congregation's baptism felt like an invasion of privacy to me. My father must have observed many baptisms as a child in Newcomb, Tennessee, where he was born and lived until his father, Matt, a lumber inspector and Baptist preacher, moved the family to Western North Carolina. One of my favorite photographs of my grandfather shows him performing a river baptism in Tennessee when he was a young, dark-haired man. In the black-and-white picture, members of his congregation—men and boys in dark pants, white shirts, and hats; women and girls in dresses and hats; and barefoot boys in overalls and floppy work hats—watch from the riverbank. Several people hold open umbrellas. My grandfather, in a long-sleeved white shirt, stands in the river, holding his right hand above his head. A woman, in a dark dress, stands with him in the water and clasps his left hand, her head bowed and her eyes closed. He looks toward the sky, and his mouth is open as if he were saying the sacred words *I now baptize thee. . . .* The picture captures the moments before my grandfather immerses the woman.

At my own baptism, though nervous, I was ready. Before the baptism began, Preacher Sprinkle explained to my Sunday school friends and me what was to happen and instructed us to hold our breath during the immersion. We could grasp his arm for support if we needed to.

Just before the ceremony, the congregation grew hushed, and my friends and I waited in an area adjoining the baptistery. When my turn came, I walked down the steps of the baptismal pool, wading into the tepid water. While I stood in the water with the preacher, he asked me if I had accepted Jesus as my personal Lord and Savior. "Yes," I said. Placing his left palm on my upper back, he lifted his right hand and pronounced the words of the sacrament: *I now baptize thee in the name of the Father and the Son and the Holy Ghost.* With my left thumb and fingers, I clipped my nostrils shut, and I closed my lips and eyes. Preacher Sprinkle covered my hand with his cupped right hand. He lowered me back into the water, and seconds later, he raised me up.

For a moment I was dazed, my long hair streaming wet at my back. My eyes burned, and I blinked to clear them. The preacher smiled as I composed myself, and I trudged through the water to ascend the steps at the other end of the pool. I went into a side room to dry off with a bath towel and change into dry clothes. I was still a little stunned, but quite proud of myself. I felt that my soul had been cleansed and, along with my family, I was a true Christian.

In the following years, my family continued to attend the same church, though a new minister would take charge. A decade after my baptism, my wedding was held in that large white sanctuary, and at that time, I questioned whether I had fully understood my actions when I was seven years old. Rededicating my life, I was baptized along with my husband on a Sunday evening. In retrospect, though, I believe my childhood conviction was genuine and that my first baptism in 1963 was probably sufficient.

A couple of years after we were baptized, my husband and I decided we would like to try a High Church service, so we started attending our local Episcopal church. We would soon be Confirmed as Episcopalians, and years later, our baby daughter would be baptized in this church—a ceremony different from the immersions I had experienced, but a meaningful one nevertheless.

When my Episcopal rector recently referred to his grandmother's "Lottie Moon Southern Baptist" persuasion, I thought of my own religious beginnings—especially my childhood baptism—and was grateful that the Baptist Church had been such an important part of my life.

Laddie

I believe I was born predisposed to love collies. And, of course, being a child in the 1960s, I grew up watching *Lassie* on TV. In fact, with my blonde pigtails, I could have passed for Timmy's sister. I was a tomboy who loved playing outdoors, climbing trees, riding my bicycle, and seeking adventures in nearby pastures and woods. All I lacked was a dog to accompany me in my adventures.

But that problem was solved one day when I entered the backyard of my uncle Lloyd, our next door neighbor. I noticed Lloyd playing with a puppy at his back stoop, so I went to investigate.

The puppy was a sable and white fur ball—a little Lassie, though actually a male puppy that I would soon name *Laddie*. Lloyd saw my immediate affection—or should I say passion—for the puppy and told me to go ask my parents if I could keep him.

I was seven and would keep him for the next ten years.

Those were good years, and Laddie was my constant companion for many of them. Most of our family photographs and our 8 mm home movies featured Laddie.

Being a collie, he was a natural herder, and I was his sheep. If I strayed near the street, he gently, but firmly took my wrist in his mouth and redirected me. One of our home movies shows me sledding down our icy, snow-covered street, Laddie running alongside, my gloved wrist in his mouth. I was never far from his sight.

But being a collie, he was also sneaky.

My paternal grandmother's house, where my family would visit on weekend afternoons, was a short drive from our neighborhood. To get to the road where she lived, we had to drive to the end of our street and then cross a two-lane highway. We shooed Laddie back as he trotted behind our Mercury. Yet he would slyly wait till we were safely out of sight and then run up the highway and cross over, someway evading traffic. When we arrived at my grandmother's house, we found Laddie resting on the front porch. My grandmother proudly said he often came to visit her. Though she was a fragile lady who didn't keep a dog or any pet of her own, she enjoyed Laddie's gentle company.

Laddie was also a digger. Once when our neighbor Virgil planted a flowering shrub, Laddie decided we needed it. He promptly dug it up and set it in our yard. My embarrassed father replanted it where Virgil had originally placed it. Virgil either didn't realize what had happened or wasn't too concerned. The shrub was not disturbed after that.

Laddie proved to be a thief more than once. One day he showed up at our house with a very large doll—a child-sized one popular at the time, its frilly dress unscathed. We had no idea what little girl he stole it from or where she lived. It probably came from my grandmother's neighborhood. Whether Laddie had brought the doll to me or just wanted it for himself, we didn't know. I think my father discarded the doll, not knowing who in the world to return it to.

In my experience through the years with the several collies I have owned, I have noted the breed's particular terror of thunderstorms.

During summer storms, at the first crash of thunder, Laddie often broke through our front screen door to get into the house. One night my mother and father were asleep in their bed, their window open to let in cool air. My father woke up to find Laddie curled up on the hardwood floor beside the bed. Apparently during a storm in the night, Laddie had jumped from the front porch through the window screen, to find shelter beside my father. He evidently knew my father slept just inside the window.

Surprisingly, I don't remember my father ever being angry at Laddie's destructive ways or threatening him. He often recalled the bedroom window incident, and in telling about it, he seemed pleased Laddie had sought him as a protector.

I think Laddie in general, though, was our protector. Insurance agents who came to our house to collect on policies feared him. I never knew of Laddie biting anyone, and all the neighbors—adults and kids—liked him, yet with his barking he could pose a fierce threat to strangers.

My mother and I sometimes turned to Laddie for solace. If we were unhappy about something, we could find him on the porch or in the yard, ready to offer his company. He would lift his paw to greet us, as if reaching out his hand in friendship. He was an understanding listener. If in some moment of mischief I scolded him, his brown eyes filled with tears, making me quickly repent my meanness. I hugged him to let him know I wasn't mad after all. He taught me compassion.

Like other collies, he understood the English language well. I could say, "Basement, boy," and he immediately headed to our cool dirt basement. It was one of his favorite places to rest.

And, not surprisingly, he chose it for his final resting place.

At seventeen, I had grown away from my era of playing with Laddie and had, in fact, married. In the early days of our marriage, my husband and I moved into his parents' home. It was here that I received an evening telephone call from my mother.

"Laddie died," she said when I answered. With emotion in her voice, she explained that my father had gone looking for Laddie and found him dead in the basement. As with all dogs I've ever known, he must have instinctively sensed what was about to happen and sought a safe, private place to die. My father quickly disposed of his body to spare my mother and me the grief of seeing him.

I told my mother, "I can't talk."

Her voice breaking too, she replied, "I can't talk either." And she hung up.

So that day I lost my friend and companion of a decade. I hope he didn't feel I had abandoned him in those teenage years when my interests turned to boys and dating and finally to marriage. My lack of attention then must have confused and saddened him. I'm sad now to think of it and wish Laddie could someway know that I love and miss him still, these forty-four years later.

The Fun We Made

As a child in Western North Carolina in the 1960s, I didn't have to look far to find ways to have fun.

Sitting in my yard on a summer day, I made flower bracelets by pulling the stem of a clover blossom through a split made in the stem of another and beading together the white flower heads. And I picked daisies to pluck out the petals to reveal *He loves me* or *He loves me not*. Fluffy dandelions were abundant and fun to blow to watch the seeds drift on the breeze.

Late spring and summer nights sparkled with lightning bugs. My mother provided a pint Mason jar, and my father punched air holes in the lid. I ran back and forth in the darkness and caught the little glowing bugs, which would not sting or bite, to collect in the jar to make a homemade lantern for my bedroom. I would keep them for a while and then set them free. Many rural children enjoyed playing with insects, especially the harmless ones like lightning bugs and green June bugs, and we looked forward to their seasonal appearance.

In those days, I loved to fish, but an afternoon of fishing didn't necessarily require the Catawba River. My backyard was my river. You didn't have to look far to find grub worm holes, and a wild onion's stalk stuck deep into the hole almost immediately produced a tug. When I pulled out the onion stalk, a plump grub worm was attached to the end. I moved from one fishing hole to another in the yard.

Whistling in different ways was fun. For instance, I blew on a blade of grass pressed between the outer edges of my thumbs and produced a shrill whistle. I also clasped my hands together, bent my thumbs, and blew into the space between my thumbs to imitate a train whistle.

My friend Mike, a boy who lived across the street, taught me to whistle through my teeth like Elly May Clampett. I learned the right position of lips and tongue to get a clear, loud whistle. At the time, I was a tomboy and proud to be able to whistle this way. I still call my border collie to his meals, as I've done with many dogs through the years, using this effective whistle.

My mother enjoys telling me about her Depression-era childhood in Clinchfield cotton mill village, where, she says, "We made our own fun."

"I loved making can-walkers," she often reminisces. She made can-walkers for me, too, using empty soup cans with twine attached for handles. Can-walkers worked like stilts to elevate you and took some getting used to. But once I stood atop the cans, gained my balance, and held the twine handles tightly enough to keep the cans snug against my feet, I paraded on my sidewalk, clomping and feeling tall.

Besides can-walkers, my mother made me a harmonica out of a comb covered in wax paper.

"You can play it like a French harp," she said and demonstrated a song for me by blowing on the side of the comb as she hummed a tune. When I played the comb, it tickled my lips, but I liked making muffled music on it.

My brother Steve and his friends on the street made their own fun, too. None of them owned a baseball, so they made one out of socks. "And we used an ax handle for a bat," Steve recalls.

Like the rest of the kids in my rural neighborhood, I owned store-bought toys—Slinkys, Yo-Yos, tops, and other treasures available at our downtown Roses five-and-dime. Yet also like them and like my mother in her cotton mill village, I created my own amusements, sometimes with the simplest resources that nature provided. The fun we made then offered a satisfaction that couldn't be found at the dime store.

Silo

That summer day in 1964 my friend Andre and I headed up our street, not knowing where our journey would take us. But the day was young and the sun beamed brightly, and we were eager for an adventure.

At the crest of the street we came to a sloping fenced pasture. Here I stretched a strand of barbed wire so Andre and I could squeeze through. Once inside the fence, we tromped through high grass and clover, pausing along the way to eat blackberries. We hiked on till we came to the end of the sun-drenched pasture and then reached the woods—shadowy and unfamiliar. We had never ventured this far before.

The woods were dense with maples, poplars, and oaks and the undergrowth thick with laurels and pine saplings. Andre and I stooped to rake back pine needles and moist black soil, hoping to uncover Indian arrowheads and other buried treasures.

As we scouted for relics, I asked Andre, "You finding anything, Andre?"

"Nah," he said, as he sat on his haunches in Bermuda shorts and concentrated on his excavating.

Andre was six years old—a cherubic boy with curly blond hair—and was a willing and imaginative companion.

After we gave up digging, we trudged on for a good while. Andre followed me—his eight-year-old leader—trusting I knew where we were going.

We reached a clearing and saw a farmhouse and barn. Nearby stood a towering shiny silo—unlike anything either of us had ever seen.

"Look at that," I told Andre, pointing to the silo, and we walked over and surveyed its expanse. "Ain't it big?" I asked. "Makes you dizzy looking up at it."

"Yeah," Andre agreed. We stood and admired the imposing domed structure. We may have had a vague idea what the silo's purpose was and what it held, but we'd never stood so close to one before, and we thought it was grand—a real treasure.

"Wonder who lives here?" I asked, nodding toward the farmhouse, and Andre shrugged. This farmstead was hidden in the woods, a good distance from our neighborhood, and was a place we'd never imagined existed.

Suddenly we heard dogs baying—hounds that seemed to be on the scent of something—probably us.

"We better go," I told Andre. "Somebody might've sicced them dogs on us."

We turned in our tracks and rushed back into the woods, which seemed darker and deeper than before.

Pushing aside tree limbs and shuffling through tangles of thorny briars that caught our bare legs, we stopped in a thicket of pines to rest.

"I ain't sure where we're at," I told Andre. "I think we're lost."

Andre didn't seem scared, though I was getting worried. What if we couldn't find our way back home?

But we pressed forward, and finally I saw a hillside ahead, washed in sunlight. "There's the pasture," I said, and we took off running.

At the fence, we slipped through the strands of barbed wire and then lunged through the grass, not slowing to sample blackberries. Our street was ahead, and we were happy to be home again.

While Andre and I were still children, his family moved off of our street and into another neighborhood in McDowell County. After he moved away, we attended different schools and lost touch. A few years ago I saw Andre's obituary in our local newspaper. When I read the tribute, I thought of the likable boy I once played with, and I grieved for that child.

Today, a four-lane, median-divided highway—US 221 Bypass—runs between the pasture and the property where the farmstead stood, and rushing traffic heading north and south has usurped the woodland that Andre and I traversed fifty-six years ago.

When I drive on the bypass, especially in late fall and winter after the leaves have fallen, I spy the old silo, its rusty frame leaning in a covering of trees. When I see it, I marvel at how far Andre and I had to walk from our street to get to it. We were so young.

The landscape of my Western North Carolina county has changed through the decades, and people I once knew and loved are gone. But the silo still stands as a reminder of a long-ago summer day and an adventure I shared with a friend.

Desk and Chair

I had spent days studying the Sears *Christmas 1964* catalog. And when I decided what I wanted to ask Santa Claus to bring me, I sat at our dining room table with a sheet of notebook paper and pencil, and in my careful third-grade cursive handwriting, I wrote:

Dear Santa,

I would like to have a Desk + Chair.
I would also like a view master Theater.
I have been very good,
I washed my mother's dishes.
and made up my bed too.
I go out and get wood.

from Julia.

In reality and regrettably, I don't remember helping my mother very much around the house throughout my childhood. I do recall going to our woodshed and helping my parents carry in sticks of wood for our dining room woodstove. But perhaps around Christmastime, I put in more effort with household chores to impress Santa with my industriousness.

By this time in my life, I had begun to write poems and short stories, usually sitting at the dining room table to do this. In making my wish list, I didn't reason that a desk and chair would be hard for Santa to manage on his sleigh, but what child questions Santa's abilities? And in our bungalow-style home, the fireplace was sealed, and a Seigler oil heater stood in front of it. So the chimney was off-limits as Santa's entry point. Yet I trusted that Santa would find a way to get my presents to me.

Thinking back on it, I seemed a bit old at eight to believe in Santa Claus, but my brother Steve and I still shared a bed, and on that Christmas Eve, we stayed awake listening and whispering about Santa's arrival.

"What's that?" I asked Steve in the darkness when I thought I heard a scratching sound on our roof.

"I think he's here," Steve said.

"Listen!" I hissed, my heart racing.

"I think he's in the front room," Steve said.

"We better be quiet, or he'll leave!" I warned.

We grew still.

I doubt Steve—twelve then—actually believed in Santa Claus, but as we lay in the chilly bedroom, huddled under our quilts to stay warm, we listened and waited, and my brother seemed as caught up in the fantasy as I was.

When we heard the cuckoo clock in the front room sounding three *cuckoos*, we decided we'd waited long enough. We jumped from our bed and bounded down the hall, passing our parents' bedroom on the way. In the front room stood our Christmas tree, a white pine which my father had cut from nearby woods and my mother and I had decorated with lights, ornaments, and silver tinsel. Underneath the tree rested colorful presents my mother had meticulously wrapped and adorned with curled ribbons and bows.

Soon my father, in boxer shorts and tee shirt, and my mother, in housecoat and hair curled in bobby pins, joined Steve and me. Neither fussed that we had roused them at three a.m.

My father had recently bought a Bell & Howell 8 mm movie camera and projector, and he recorded my brother and me opening our presents. In fact, this filming of Christmas, 1964, was the first in a series of home movies he would take throughout my childhood. Indeed, much of what I remember about this particular Christmas is due to his documenting the holiday on film.

In my pajamas and barefoot, I excitedly tore into my presents. One of them was a Chatty Cathy doll—a present from my uncle Junior. I held up the doll for my father to film and pulled its string a couple of times to hear what it had to say. I then found the package containing my Tru-Vue Projection Theatre, a variation of the View-Master Theater I had listed on my Santa letter. What a great present it was, too. Every night I would lie in bed, insert the color slides into the red-and-white plastic projector, and project Walt Disney cartoon scenes onto the wall for my brother and me to see. After Steve moved into a bedroom upstairs, I shared the cartoons with girlfriends who spent the night.

Finally, I discovered my desk and chair. Ironically, I had been setting packages on the desk, not realizing what I was using for a table. My mother or father must have said, "Do you like your desk?" and made me aware of it. When I realized what was in front of me, I pulled out the chair and sat on its beige vinyl seat. Steve opened the desk drawer, and I looked inside and then closed it. I admired the wooden desk's shiny finish and felt proud to have a desk of my own. In the years to come, I would sit at that desk in my bedroom and let my imagination run free as I read books like *Black Beauty* and *Heidi* and wrote poems and stories filled with dreams and adventures.

Christmas of 1964 would be my last one that included Santa Clause. I didn't want to stop believing in him and held fiercely to my faith as long as I could. But by the fourth grade, other kids had stopped believing and scoffed at the believers. So I, too, let Santa Claus go. And Christmas was never the same again.

I didn't write any more letters to Santa, but I'm grateful my mother kept my final one that I can now read and treasure.

Soon after that Christmas, the street where I lived changed, too. My uncle Lloyd—my father's younger brother and our next door neighbor— died in May 1965, and his untimely death at forty-four brought grief into our family and a void into our close-knit neighborhood. The winter before Lloyd's death, my father was outside with his Bell & Howell camera filming a deep snow that had blanketed our Western North Carolina county. I was sliding down the icy street, my collie, Laddie, running alongside me, and Steve, my mother, and our neighbors from across the street were frolicking in the snow, throwing snowballs at each other. While my father filmed us, Lloyd came trudging through his yard, heading to his car parked in the driveway below his house. He saw my father aiming the camera at him, and he waved. A few months later when my family watched this home movie on the projection screen set up in our front room, we were sad but grateful Lloyd had happened to be outside in the snow that day. The fact that he was captured on film has helped me remember him through the years.

Unfortunately, my Tru-Vue projector eventually stopped working—its bulb burning out—and was discarded. After that, my bedroom wall stayed dark at night.

But I still have my desk and chair. I keep it safely stored, covered by a patchwork quilt. Though I don't sit at it anymore when I write my poems and stories, I'm in no hurry to let it go.

My Mother's Snow Cream

In my childhood, I loved waking up on winter mornings to see the world sparkling white with snowflakes swirling. It was a magical sight.

On those snowy days, the kids in my McDowell County neighborhood congregated to slide down our icy street on makeshift sleds and splatter each other in snowball free-for-alls. Sometimes our parents joined in the fun. But besides playing in the snow, I looked forward to a treat that came with the wintry weather: my mother's snow cream.

After a deep snowfall, my mother would say, "Go get me a pan of snow."

Bundled up in hooded sweater, rubber boots, and gloves, I took off with a dishpan to our backyard, where pure, untouched billows waited; and with a large spoon I skimmed swaths of snow into the pan, packing it to the brim.

Once back inside the warm kitchen, my snow garb shed, I set the pan on the counter beside the sink, where my mother had already gathered a can of Carnation Evaporated Milk, a bag of granulated sugar, and a bottle of vanilla extract.

"Get me my mixer," she said.

Happily, I retrieved the Sunbeam hand mixer, inserted the beaters, and plugged it in for her.

Into a large bowl, she spooned mounds of snow, poured creamy evaporated milk on it, and began beating. As she whipped the mixture, she added more snow, sugar, and a slosh of vanilla until the bowl teemed with a smooth, crystalline confection.

"I can make it chocolate," she offered and glanced toward the Hershey's Cocoa tin in the cupboard.

"No, that's okay," I said, preferring to leave it vanilla.

We filled two dessert bowls and stuck teaspoons in them for me to carry to my father and brother who watched television in the front room. I hurried back to the kitchen to fill my bowl.

"I wouldn't eat too much," my mother cautioned. "It might give you a sore throat." She always issued this warning when she made snow cream for us.

Our family didn't seem to worry about eating snow from the first snowfall, as some people did. And I don't recall getting a sore throat from eating snow—either in my mother's snow cream or in the handfuls I'd scoop from the yard to sample.

The last snow cream I remember my mother making was in mid-March 1993, after a blizzard that dumped eighteen inches of snow on Marion and kept us trapped inside our houses for a week. My husband, Steve, and I lived in a rural community near the mountains, and during the power outage that week, we depended on the creek for water, a fireplace for heat, and oil lamps for light.

When the highway was passable, Steve drove me in his Dodge Dakota to my parents' house, where I grew up. The power in their area, closer to town than ours, had been restored, and I looked forward to getting to their house and the comfort it promised.

My mother's dining room was warm and pungent with the scent of burning oak from her woodstove. While I sat at her table, she brought me a tall glass filled with snow cream and an iced tea spoon to eat it with.

"I hoped you'd make some snow cream," I said. I believe she made it especially for me.

It was the tastiest snow cream I'd ever eaten on one of the most memorable days of my life. I had missed seeing my parents, now in their seventies, and had worried about their safety during the blizzard. And frankly I felt like I'd been released from captivity after a week of isolation.

"This is so good," I said as I spooned the icy treat into my mouth and savored the sweet vanilla flavor.

"I hope it don't give you a sore throat," my mother said.

"It won't," I assured her, intending to eat every bite.

And that's exactly what I did that March day, as I'd always done all those magical snowy days of my childhood.

House Next Door

My uncle Lloyd died of a massive heart attack when he was forty-four years old. It was May 14, 1965, and I had turned nine the month before.

Lloyd was my father's younger brother, and he and his wife, Jewell, lived in the house next door to my family. So on that day in May we lost not only our kin, but also our next door neighbor. Such a loss in our rural North Carolina neighborhood was great because the families on our street were close. Like the close-knit residents of Mayberry on *The Andy Griffith Show,* most of the folks in my neighborhood attended the same community church, the children went to the same school and played together, and we constantly visited each other's houses. Neighbors joined for Sunday afternoon picnics or even weekend trips to Myrtle Beach. We ate out together. In fact, a couple of days before Lloyd's death, he, Jewell, and my family shared a meal at our local Pilot House Restaurant. During this time, Petula Clark's song "Downtown" was the number one hit, and it played on the car radio during our drive back home.

A good-looking man who favored the actor Robert Young and was affectionately nicknamed "Peach," Lloyd was a World War II Army veteran, straight-laced, and dedicated to our Baptist church. He was our choir director and a Sunday school department head. He was also a skilled organist. He had a spinet organ in his living room, which he once showed me how to play. I always thought it unique that he owned an organ. Most families then had an upright piano in their house, but rarely an organ.

He was a good uncle. Though he and Jewell had no children, he seemed to enjoy my company. He gave me a little job of finding lost golf balls he'd putted in his backyard and paid me a dime per recovered ball. This was good money for a child. But most importantly, he gave me one of the most meaningful gifts of my life. When I was seven and started into his backyard to play, as I often did, I noticed that he was standing at his back stoop, a sable and white collie puppy frolicking about his feet. At the time my favorite television show was *Lassie*, so I raced to see the puppy. Lloyd saw my excitement and put the puppy in my arms. As I nuzzled my face in its soft neck and savored its puppy aroma, Lloyd said, "Would you like to have that puppy?"

I couldn't believe what he was asking.

"Yes!" I said.

"Well, go ask your mama and daddy."

I ran home to ask and quickly went back to get the puppy. I named him *Laddie*, and he would be my constant companion for many years.

On the morning of Lloyd's death, my mother was in Jewell's kitchen, applying a color treatment to Jewell's hair. Around eight o'clock, Lloyd came home unexpectedly from his job as a supervisor at Broyhill Furniture plant. He went straight to his bedroom and lay down. It was odd for Lloyd to come home this way. Like my father with his hosiery mill job, Lloyd took his furniture plant job seriously and must have hated leaving his workers unsupervised.

Jewell and my mother heard a strange noise, as if Lloyd were in distress. Jewell went to the bedroom to see what was wrong.

Soon she came back into the kitchen and exclaimed, "He's dead!" Apparently, he had died before she reached him.

Frantic, her hair still wet with the color solution, Jewell rushed across the street to get our older neighbor Neal. Neal immediately called McCall's Funeral Home, which sent an ambulance to get Lloyd's body. According to Lloyd's death certificate, he died at home at 8:15 a.m.

I've always been troubled by Lloyd's premature death. For years I've heard the same story: the day before he died, Lloyd had been to the hospital for medical tests, and, according to my mother, "He had been sent away with a clean bill of health."

But, obviously, something was not right.

In going through my grandmother's old letters, I found one that my aunt—my father's younger sister—had written to my grandmother from Sacramento, California, where she lived at the time. The letter was dated March 29, 1965—six and a half weeks before Lloyd's death. She wrote: "I'm glad there wasn't too much wrong with Lloyd's stomach."

My mother, too, has remarked that before his death, Lloyd "had been sick with stomach problems."

Like Lloyd, my maternal grandmother received a dismissive diagnosis when she grew ill in 1962. Suffering from back and chest pain, she sought a doctor's help. He came to her house, examined her, and concluded that the cause of her pain was "chronic neuritis." As it turned out, she had actually suffered a heart attack. The next day she was taken to the hospital where she died.

Lloyd's death certificate states that his immediate cause of death was "massive coronary occlusion," and the antecedent cause was "myocardial infarction."

Upon further investigation, I have found that the symptoms of myocardial infarction include nausea and vomiting—symptoms that might be mistaken for acute indigestion.

So I believe that Lloyd's doctor, like my grandmother's doctor three years earlier, did not detect his severe heart problem, perhaps misdiagnosing his symptoms as indigestion and erroneously sending him home "with a clean bill of health." When Jewell heard the noise in the bedroom and went to see what was wrong, she was totally unaware of Lloyd's dire heart condition. His death certificate states that the interval between the onset of his heart attack and his death was six minutes. It's no wonder she didn't get there in time.

That first night after Lloyd's death, Jewell was distraught, probably still in shock, and didn't want to stay in the house alone. My mother stayed with her.

As was still the custom at that time, my uncle's body was brought home to lie in state. His open casket was set up in the living room, where family, friends, neighbors, and church members gathered to view his body and pay their respects. Women brought an abundance of food to Jewell's kitchen for anyone who might be hungry.

After the funeral at our church, Lloyd was buried at McDowell Memorial Park, a recently established cemetery on the outskirts of town.

Following the burial, Jewell continued to feel uneasy about staying alone at night. Her own family lived some distance away in the mountains of Yancey County. My first cousins, two sisters aged seven and eleven, volunteered to spend one night. They arrived early that spring evening, and we played outside till dark. My mother stayed another night.

But one weekend morning my mother said, "Jewell asked if you would spend the night with her tonight."

I imagined that my two cousins might be there again, and it would be a sort of pajama party.

"Yes," I said.

As the afternoon passed and evening came, I realized that my cousins were not coming. I began to fret and dread the sunset. I dared not go outside to play for fear Jewell might see me and call me up there. The thought of being trapped all night in a lonely house with an aunt I didn't really know that well tormented me.

I made no moves to prepare for my overnight stay. Around dusk I sneaked on my pajamas and slipped into bed. My parents were down the hall in the front room watching television. My brother Steve was still outside playing with friends. In a while, my mother, who must have been looking for me, came into my bedroom.

"Julia," she said, "you ain't gone to bed, have you? Ain't you going up to Jewell's to spend the night? You said you would."

Playing possum, I shifted and pretended to rouse. I mumbled, "I'm already asleep." Burrowing deeper under my covers, I rolled over to face the wall. I hoped my mother couldn't hear my heart thumping.

She quietly left my room and went up to Jewell's house herself. She never scolded me for going back on my word. She must have understood how I felt.

To my relief, Jewell never asked me again to stay overnight. In time, she left our street, moving back home to Micaville in Yancey County. For a short period, she rented her vacant house and then sold it to my older brother Butch and his wife. So once more we had kin living next door.

Jewell never remarried, and when she died in 2009, she was brought back to McDowell County to be laid to rest beside Lloyd at Memorial Park.

Today, my nephew and his family live in the house that once belonged to my uncle Lloyd. When I look at it, I remember the days when I played in his backyard, Laddie by my side. But I also recall a promise that I broke to a grieving widow who did not want to stay there alone.

Like the song "Downtown," the house reminds me of a sad moment in my family's history.

Saturdays at the Mill

From as early as I can recall, my father and mother both worked in a hosiery mill. He was a machine fixer and she a knitter. Though they didn't always work at the same mill, occasionally they did, and for a while they worked together at Broadway Hosiery Mill on East Court Street in Marion, the town where I grew up and still live. Sometimes they worked on Saturdays, and when they did, I came with them.

In the mill, the warm air smelled of machine oil and cotton dust, and the knitting machines chattered continuously. But to me, the heat, odor, and noise seemed natural and didn't deter my enjoyment.

On Saturdays, the few workers seemed to take little notice of me, so I had the run of the place. I would jump into a pile of white socks, soft and linty, spreading them asunder and raking them over me like a blanket. And I'd play with my father's bench vise, testing its pressure by placing my hand between the cool, oily jaws and turning the handle. Occasionally I would clamp too tight and mash my fingers, but the discomfort didn't faze me.

When my mother reminisces about this mill, she recalls, "I liked it because we was close to town, practically in town"—and that's also why I liked it best of all the mills my parents worked in.

One of the charms of the mill's location was its proximity to the town's cinema—the House Theatre—where my mother sometimes took me to see a Disney movie. On Saturdays when I grew restless in the mill, I would wander outside and look up the street where I could see moviegoers entering the theater for the matinee. One such day I spied my school friend Kathy and some other kids congregated in front of the theater. They were all dressed up and went in together. I hadn't been invited to Kathy's birthday party this year, as I had been the last, and I watched the celebrants from afar, feeling dejected.

Maybe I mentioned this disappointment to my parents, because on a Saturday after that, one of them said, "Why don't you go to the movies today?" The marquee announced *The Three Lives of Thomasina*, which my mother hadn't taken me to see yet.

I was delighted. With the money my father gave me, I walked up the sidewalk, crossed the street, and bought my ticket at the booth outside. I entered the theater, stopped at the lobby's concession stand for a snack, and went into the dark auditorium. Parents and children were already settled in their seats. I took mine, feeling a little peculiar to be sitting by myself, but I wasn't afraid. I felt courageous and proud that my parents had given me this opportunity.

A few months later, I was standing in the school lunch line when I noticed the principal and a teacher having a conversation. I overheard the words "fire in town" and felt a sense of dread. Someway, I knew my parents' mill was involved.

That evening when I came home, I learned that a blaze had started in Seagle Feed and Seed Store that adjoined the mill, and it quickly spread. Today, my mother remembers that the mill workers were alerted to the fire by heat emanating from a wall between the businesses. "We seen bricks getting red-hot," she says. "I grabbed the lunch I'd packed, but my pretty blue coat burned up." Through the years, she has often lamented losing this wool coat that matched the color of her eyes.

(Recently, I learned from Harold Seagle, who was assisting his uncle in the family's feed and seed store that day, that the cause of the fire was presumably a spark created in the grinding mill—probably from a nail or other piece of metal that had originated in dried corn stalks being shoveled into the grinding mill. The spark ignited dust and caused an explosion and an ensuing fireball that reached the store's ceiling and set dust on the timbers on fire. At this point, Harold ran next door to the hosiery mill—a part of the same building—and told the workers, including my parents, to get out. Harold related, "There was a lot of fertilizer containing nitrogen in the storage area of the store, and when the fire started to burn hot, the fertilizer started to explode. The fire was so hot and the explosions so violent that the fire department had to fight the fire from a distance." Naturally, when I learned these details, I was horrified at how dire my parents' situation had been that day.)

Soon after the fire, my father went back to the rubble to recover his toolbox. He brought it home to show my mother, brother, and me, and when he rummaged through the charred tools, his troubled face and quavering voice betrayed his hurt feelings. A former Merchant Marine who had served in World War II, he was a tough man, usually reserved in his emotions. This day, however, I saw a different side of him, and his sadness made me sad, too.

The fire in 1965 destroyed more than a favorite coat and a valued toolbox. It stole from my parents a workplace that they genuinely liked and the livelihood that it provided for our family. Of course, my parents found new jobs, as hosiery mills were plentiful in our area then.

Still there would never be another mill that I enjoyed so much as I did Broadway Hosiery Mill. I won't forget those Saturdays when I jumped into a pile of socks or played with my father's vise or ventured alone to a movie theater. The fire took the mill away, but it didn't steal my memories of a special place and time.

A Horse of My Own

One of my first toys was a Quick Draw McGraw doll. He was a blue stuffed horse with white hooves and a soft vinyl face. He had big blue eyes and a friendly red smile. I called him *Quickie* and spoke for him, like a ventriloquist, and we talked to each other.

One day my family drove from my Western North Carolina hometown, Marion, to Drexel, thirty miles away, to visit relatives. Quickie came along, riding in my lap. Later that day when we arrived back home, I realized I had left Quickie behind in Drexel. I was lonely without him and relieved when my aunt and uncle brought him home to me a week later. But I was also ashamed to face him.

At my sixth birthday party in 1962, I sat at the head of the dining room table with my brother Steve while my guests stood around waiting for me to blow out my birthday candles. Quickie was there with me, a birthday hat on his head.

During my girlhood, I loved reading about horses. Some favorite books were *Album of Horses, Black Beauty*, and *All Horses Go to Heaven.* On sunny days, I would spread a blanket in our yard, pile my books around me, and read horse stories. These stories taught me about different breeds and told tales of courageous horses. I wrote my own horse stories, too. My first one "The Story of a Jockey" concerned a girl who finds a wild white stallion, tames him, and rides him in a horserace.

I liked to draw horses, following the steps in my *Jon Gnagy Learn to Draw* book. I kept a notebook of my drawings, and in a separate scrapbook I pasted horse-related pictures and articles I found in *Asheville Citizen-Times* and *Parade.* These clippings featured common horses and famous ones, like the racehorse Kelso.

I collected model horses that my mother bought for me at Roses five-and-dime store. This collection included many breeds and colors: bays, buckskins, palominos, pintos, and dapple grays. Two were outfitted with fancy Western saddles and bridles. I spent hours admiring and playing with my model horses.

When my family traveled to the Cherokee Indian Reservation for a weekend vacation, my father always stopped along the way at a roadside riding stable to allow me a trail ride. Riding one of the old horses through the woods, a teenage guide leading us on his horse, was the highlight of the trip for me.

But what I longed for was a horse of my own to love and take care of. I begged my father, "If you'll get me a horse, I won't ask for anything else the rest of my life."

My dream came true when I was ten and a fifth grader. My parents took me to a farm in Morganton, a neighboring town, to look at a Shetland pony we had heard about. I rode the black pony down a dirt road at the farm. But on the ride back, I noticed a pale horse in a pasture. He was a young Appaloosa-Quarter Horse cross, named *Thunder*, and when I rode him, my mind was made up. My father paid the farmer one hundred dollars, and our neighbor David hauled Thunder for us in the bed of his pickup truck. Our barn and fence weren't finished yet, so David kept him in his pasture for a while. But soon I was able to bring him home.

In the next few years, I spent a lot of time with Thunder—feeding him, brushing him, and riding him. We had many adventures together. One summer day as I rode him in my front yard, I noticed a copperhead stretched on the cement walk. I was afraid if Thunder saw the snake, he would spook and run wild with me, so I turned him quickly and cantered back to the corral. On a winter day, during a heavy snowfall, I rode him bareback in the field below our house. When I felt his hooves slipping, I grasped his wet mane. Yet I knew if I fell off, I would land in the soft snow. So we trotted joyously, snowflakes swirling around like the inside of a snow globe.

Those years with Thunder were dear ones, and I will never forget him. The bond between a girl and her horse is special—unlike any other. I'm grateful I had a horse of my own so I could experience such a friendship.

The Party

The houses in my working-class neighborhood were one- or two-story wood frame homes with neat front yards. Some neighbors had vegetable gardens in side yards and fenced in back pastures with a barn, a woodshed, a milk cow or coop of chickens. We all had wells for water, and by the mid-1960s, everyone had an inside toilet, though a few outhouses still stood.

My family's home was a two-story house with gray asbestos shingle siding, a large front porch, a wide cement walk that led from the porch steps to the street, and ample front, side, and back yards that my mother adorned with fragrant, colorful flower beds and decorative wooden border fences. Elm, poplar, maple, and apple trees provided shade, and our lower side yard was large enough to accommodate my brother Steve's baseball games with the neighborhood boys. The upper end of our backyard was enclosed by a white-washed wooden corral and contained a red barn for my horse, Thunder. An adjoining plot of woods was fenced with barbed wire for Thunder to roam in.

Though located a short drive from town, our neighborhood retained a rural quality and was a safe and fun place in which to live. Children of all ages and both sexes were abundant, so I never lacked playmates. The adults were friendly, more like communal parents. Many of us attended the same community Baptist church, and the kids frequently went in and out of each other's houses, sharing meals and spending the night.

Every family, except the elderly ones, had a dog. Through the years, there was my collie, Laddie, and our border collie mix, Loonie, a stray that we took in. She became Laddie's mate and whelped eight healthy puppies, which quickly found new homes. Other neighborhood dogs included Tramp, a terrier; Lucy, a cocker spaniel; Cleo, a beagle; and Buster, a German shepherd. Buster was a vicious and feared dog that was said to have bit off the ear of a child. We all kept vigilant for Buster when we walked down the sloping street, passing the hillside where Buster and his owners lived, to get to our school bus stop at the highway. But otherwise, the dogs and people all got along happily.

Our neighborhood began to change when two one-story duplex apartment buildings were constructed across the street from Thunder's woods. The apartments were built by a businessman Gene, who, for a while, lived in one of the units with his wife. Besides being in the construction business, Gene was also a pilot and flying instructor for our local airport. He often flew his private airplane over our community and offered rides to folks in our neighborhood. My brother Steve and his buddy Joe, who lived across the street from us, took a ride once, and Gene flew the plane upside down in some trick flying. Other neighbors commented about how interesting our neighborhood looked from the air, everyone's property neatly blocked off. Though I never rode in Gene's airplane, I enjoyed seeing him fly over the street and waved at him as he passed overhead.

Gene was a congenial man who walked across the street from his apartment and stood at Thunder's barbed wire fence, feeding him vegetable scraps. Gene was well-liked, and I don't recall anyone remarking negatively about the apartments or resenting his bringing a new kind of housing into our traditional neighborhood.

Gene's two duplex apartment buildings were brick structures, each unit containing a wide picture window, a front entrance door, and a side door at the carport. The apartments were modern, stark, and efficient—typical of the minimalist style of the 1960s.

The tenants never mingled with the rest of us, though we kids used the apartments' level paved entranceway and sloping driveways for our bicycle turnarounds. I could really pick up speed there on my blue Western Flyer bike. Tenants came and went, and I never knew any of them. They were couples or single people, it seemed, with no children evident. I never entered any of the four apartments, but I did have an occasion to get a glimpse inside one of them.

It was Halloween in the mid-1960s, and my next door neighbor Katie and I began our trek around the block to trick or treat. We had already begun celebrating the season by transforming an upstairs bedroom of my house into a "haunted house." With Katie's direction, we hung an old white bed sheet, streaked with red paint borrowed from my Paint-by-Number Kit, across the room. This "blood"-stained sheet was our entrance curtain. Behind this we cluttered the floor with my troll dolls, model horses, and stuffed animals as if they were victims of some perverse captor.

We sat on the bed and plotted how to make the room scarier, but quickly grew bored with our project, and Katie went home.

My mother came upstairs to see what we'd been up to. She looked around the room and shook her head.

"Don't you and Katie ever tear up this room like this again," she said. And she expressed her disapproval that Katie had left me with a mess to clean up by myself.

"We won't," I said, and we didn't.

It didn't take me long to realize that Katie could be creative, but mischievous at times, such as this one.

For our trick or treat jaunt, I had dressed like a hobo, wearing ragged pants, my brother's cast off plaid wool jacket, and a floppy hat. I believe Katie wore her Junior Girl Scout uniform, of which she was so proud.

Katie's family rented the house of my late uncle Lloyd. His wife, Jewell, didn't want to live alone after Lloyd died unexpectedly, so she moved home to a mountain county where her family lived. When we gained new next door neighbors, I was delighted this family included a girl my age.

Though a couple of years shy of being a teenager, Katie looked thirteen—tall and willowy with shoulder-length dark hair, blue eyes, and a heart-shaped face. She reminded me then of Elizabeth Taylor in *National Velvet*. My jealousy of her slender build and pretty looks was balanced by admiration for her outgoing personality and pleasure in her company.

Every Halloween, certain neighbors dropped the same treats into one's bag. This year was no exception: an unwrapped chocolate-frosted cupcake from Georgie, a handful of popcorn from Marie, another handful from Cora, more popcorn from Ruby, a still-warm chocolate chip cookie from Dora, a few rare candy bars, and so on. By the end of the evening, our brown grocery bags held a mix of the salty and sweet, all stuck together in a gooey mess to be sorted out and eaten later.

Tonight we decided to try a new destination that had never been approached. Walking down the steep street by Thunder's woods, we noticed bright lights shining through the curtains of the picture window of one of the apartments. Cars lined the driveway, and music blared from inside.

The apartments might have been considered off limits to our trick or treating since we didn't know the families living there. But in the past, this circumstance of approaching strangers' houses had never stopped the kids on my street from trooping across the highway at the foot of our street and prowling into different neighborhoods, such as the one where my grandmother lived, which were within a reasonable walking distance. So when Katie and I saw lights and heard music at the apartment, she was game to stop there and so was I.

We went to the door, and Katie tapped. No one responded, the music drowning out her tentative taps. She knocked again, this time harder, and a man—probably in his thirties—opened the door. He looked at us, glassy-eyed, and smiled as if he didn't quite recognize his newly arrived guests. Together Katie and I yelled, "Trick or treat!" A little unsteady on his feet, he said enthusiastically, "Come in!"

Glancing inside the neat, sparsely furnished front room, we saw men and women mingling, glasses in their hands. I didn't notice anyone wearing a Halloween costume. The scene reminded me of an episode of *Bewitched*—urbane and chic.

Neither Katie nor I was naïve about alcohol drinking or drunkenness. Though my neighborhood was basically a sober one—most of us being members of the same Southern Baptist church, which made clear its rule about forbidding consumption of alcoholic beverages (a sign in the vestibule stating this covenant)—a few families kept grapevines on their property and privately made homemade wine. Some momentary backsliding to sneak a can of Schlitz into a weekend's relaxation was not unheard of. And a recent Sunday night intrusion into our home by an intoxicated man, who had wandered up the street to beg a cigarette from my father, had been an unsettling reminder of the realities of alcohol abuse. Tragically this man would die in a house fire shortly after his intrusion. He was rumored to have fallen asleep while smoking in bed after an alcoholic binge.

Yet this incident was extraordinary. Our town was dry then, and our neighborhood discreet. Even the few drinkers who would have to go to a bootlegger or drive out of town to Morganton or Black Mountain to get a "package" wouldn't dream of sitting on a front porch with a beer can in hand. And, truly, most of our neighbors simply did not drink. I'm sure of this, as I was in their houses enough, day and night, to be familiar with their habits.

So to see the apartment tenant so happily tipsy, his guests unapologetically enjoying their drinks, surprised Katie and me.

She and I stood mute.

The man laughed, his brown hair disheveled and falling onto his brow. He looked at our grocery bags that we had thrust forward and at our outfits. Soon he realized we were not coming inside and connected why we had yelled "Trick or treat!"

He reached into his pants pocket and pulled out a fistful of change. He managed to drop some coins into each of our bags.

"Thank you," we said, and he nodded, clearly amused by our visit, and closed the door behind us.

Well, I thought, he must be a "swinger," and this was his "pad." Only in movies or in TV sitcoms had I seen such a scenario as his party. Only in a mod apartment would such a person live—at least in my neighborhood.

As far as I know, I never saw this man face-to-face again. I never learned his name. He may have lived in the apartment for a while, but he kept to himself, and I went about my business of associating only with the regular neighbors.

Since then, the neighborhood has continued to change. Houses have been remodeled, modernized, upgraded. Vinyl siding has replaced old exteriors; carports added; barns and chicken coops demolished; fencing removed, woods cleared, and pastures mown to make manicured lawns.

New faces have replaced the old familiar ones as new residents have moved into homes long occupied by others. Children are few and dogs scarce.

Katie didn't remain my next door neighbor for long. My aunt Jewell decided to sell her house to my brother Butch, so Katie's family moved to town. I visited her there a couple of times, but our friendship faded.

The apartments still stand, oddly unchanged—a remnant of the 1960s. Gene, their builder and an early occupant, passed away in 2016. A decade ago, while I visited a family member at Autumn Care, a local nursing home, I saw Gene spending time with the residents there. He regularly sent bouquets of roses to the elderly ladies who lived there. I thought this gesture unusually kind and imagined what the flowers must have meant to their recipients.

I don't know whether Gene still owned the apartments then, and I have no idea who owns them now. But when I see them today, I'm taken back to the 1960s again when a little hobo stood beside her Girl Scout friend, waiting for a door to open to an unfamiliar but very memorable world.

My Christmas, 1967

Our strings of colored lights were worn, some paint chipped off the bulbs. But they burned bright, and the needles of our white pine tree—freshly cut by my father—stuck to the hot bulbs and tinged our front room with a piney fragrance. On the limbs my mother and I hung shiny glass balls and bells and grape clusters. At the peak she secured an old fluted tin topper that featured a Santa Claus face with a spun glass beard. We finished by coating the tree with silver tinsel.

I had scouted out a Silvertone flat-top guitar in the Sears *Christmas 1967* catalog and had dropped hints to my parents, showing them the ad in the catalog. Of course, at eleven years old I didn't believe in Santa Claus, so I couldn't turn to him for help. As a matter of fact, I had recently entered a new phase of my life, going from a child obsessed with horses to a pre-teen enthralled by the Monkees. I loved their TV show, their records, and *Monkee Spectacular* magazine. In my diary I bragged that "I got over 45 pictures of the Monkees on my wall." That December my favorite song was "Daydream Believer," and I played the single continuously on my brother Steve's portable record player.

My family did much of our Christmas shopping at the Sears store in downtown Asheville, a thirty mile drive from my hometown, Marion. So on a Saturday in mid-December, we traveled to Buncombe County for our annual holiday shopping trip there. Once we had parked at Sears, we headed up the street to the S&W Cafeteria.

The S&W was a historic landmark in downtown Asheville, known for its lavish Art Deco facade, elegant interior, and tasty food. Anytime we visited Asheville, we ate at the S&W. On this Saturday in December, we chose our dishes and carried our trays upstairs to the mezzanine. We found a table near the windows that offered a view of the city.

While I ate my meal, I noticed people at other tables. At one, a priest in his black clergy shirt and white collar sat with some nuns in dark habits. Before they ate, they prayed and crossed themselves. Only at this cafeteria did I see Roman Catholics, my family being Baptist, and I was impressed by their reverent behavior.

After our meal, we returned to Sears, where my parents told me to stay put in one spot while they shopped across the room.

"Don't be looking around," my mother said. "Stay right here till we get back." Then she and my father took off together. I hoped they were going after my guitar.

Despite myself, I couldn't help but look around to see my father carrying the Silvertone guitar I'd admired in the Sears catalog. I was ashamed I'd seen him sneaking it to a cash register, but happy to know I would get the present I wanted.

Once my parents and I were together again, my father bought us a bag of chocolate-covered peanuts to take home and eat later. But before we left, he pointed to a sign announcing that John Parris was in the store signing copies of his latest book *Mountain Bred*.

"Can we go see him?" I asked, and my father said, "Yeah."

Every Sunday, my father and I sat together and read the *Asheville Citizen-Times*. We first removed the funny papers and looked at the comic strips, his favorite being *Andy Capp*. He liked the English working-class characters that likely stirred his memories of being in England during World War II. After we perused the funnies, we found John Parris' column "Roaming the Mountains," one in which the author told tales of Western North Carolina mountain people and their traditions. As my father read the column aloud, I listened intently. His deep, expressive voice made the story come to life, and he took pleasure in reading it to me.

"Let's go find him," my father said.

When we saw Parris sitting at a table with a display of books, I whispered, "There he is!" I recognized him from his picture that always accompanied his column.

In suit and tie and with gray hair and neat mustache, Parris was a distinguished-looking gentleman who seemed to me very refined.

I was bashful and hesitant to approach him.

My father walked with me to the table, but once there, he took a step back to allow me the author's attention.

Parris greeted me and asked where I was from.

"Marion," I replied, and I'm sure even in that one word he could hear my accent.

He told me he was from the mountains, too. His kind manner put me at ease, and I explained I'd seen his stories in the newspaper. He seemed pleased that I was familiar with his writing.

"I want to get her one of your books," my father said, and Parris asked if I would like him to sign it for me.

"Yes," I said and watched him as he picked up a book, opened it, and put his pen to the first page.

When he finished writing, he handed the book to me, and I held it against my chest, proud to have an autographed copy. I couldn't wait to see what he had written.

At home, my father and I read the inscription that Parris had penned in a clear cursive hand:

To Julia Nunnally—

*Who is mountain
bred, too, and who
has a proud heritage.
Best of good wishes—*
*John Parris
Sylva N.C.
Dec. 16, 1967*

Of course, I still have that signed copy of *Mountain Bred*, its dust jacket now discolored and worn. I'm grateful the jacket's backside features an author photograph in which Parris sits at a typewriter, a bookcase behind him, a tobacco pipe in his hand, and a warm smile on his face. This image sparks the memory of my Christmastime conversation with him when I was eleven—a meeting that surely influenced my desire to become an author. And it reminds me of the Sunday mornings when my father and I shared a newspaper, laughing at the funnies and enjoying an Appalachian tale.

Besides being my first time meeting an author, that Christmas was a first for other things, as well. My parents, Steve, and I drove to Fort Lauderdale, Florida, to spend the holiday with my uncle Glenn and his family. We left rural Western North Carolina on a wintry morning with snow in the air to arrive the next day in a warm, green suburb. This spur-of-the-moment vacation was fun, but when Steve and I reminisce about it today, he says, "I missed being at home for Christmas." "I did too," I admit. It just didn't feel like Christmas in Florida.

Before we left for Florida, we opened our presents. I feigned surprise at my guitar, and my father tuned it for me and my mother showed me a few chords. The glossy mahogany-toned guitar came with a pick, an instruction booklet, and a how-to-play record. So I was set.

I soon learned, however, that I was not cut out to be a guitarist. My fingertips became sore from pressing the strings, and some chords were too difficult for me to play, so I gave up. But I would begin taking piano lessons the following year and find my true musical talent.

Most of the Christmas decorations from my childhood are long gone though I still have a few of the glass ornaments, which I hang on my family's Fraser fir every year.

But I have many memories of that time: a pine tree brightly lit and covered with tinsel; a song I loved and a guitar I longed to have but never learned to play; a writer I admired, whom my father allowed me to meet; and a bittersweet journey away from home.

This was my Christmas, 1967.

The Cherokee Sweethearts

When I was a girl, my parents and I would drive two hours to Cherokee in the mountains of Western North Carolina for a summer weekend getaway. This was in the 1960s, long before the Cherokee Indian Reservation transformed to feature the glitzy Harrah's Cherokee Casino Resort. Instead, the reservation offered tourists a main drag of small gift shops that sold deerskin and elkskin moccasins, feathered headdresses, toy bow and arrow sets, Oconaluftee Indian Village crafts, Kodak film, risqué car tags, and delicate souvenirs, including snow globes with miniature black bears, which I couldn't resist shaking to make the snow swirl. Outside on the street one could find a costumed "Indian chief" who was available for pictures for a small fee. A sideshow exhibit "The World's Smallest Horse" was set up in an enclosed area near the shops.

Along with the gift shops were sit-down restaurants, such as the spacious, air-conditioned Sequoyah Restaurant, and other cafés and restaurants that beckoned tourists with Pet and Sealtest ice cream signs. My family usually grabbed a hot dog and soft drink at one of the less fancy eating places and ice cream at the Dairy Queen.

Generally, my parents and I found a room at the Broken Arrow Motel, a budget motel just off the highway before we reached the reservation. The accommodations here were a small room with two double beds, a dresser, a black-and-white television set, and an adjoining bathroom. We enjoyed the room's refreshing coolness, its air conditioning a luxury we didn't have at home. And though the television set didn't work well, its picture rolling despite my father's efforts to adjust it, we loved kicking off our shoes, stretching out on the beds, watching a movie on TV, and drinking ice-cold bottles of Orange Crush from the vending machine outside.

One Friday evening, after my parents were finished with their hosiery mill work for the week, we took off for our weekend jaunt to the Smoky Mountains. As always, when we reached Maggie Valley, we stopped at a roadside riding stable to indulge me a horseback ride and then ate supper at our favorite country café. But as we proceeded to Cherokee, we couldn't find a vacancy at the Broken Arrow Motel or even in the seedy tourist cabins farther along. So we drove on, hoping to find a room. Arriving at the reservation after dark, we saw a lighted area up ahead where a crowd had gathered, and we heard amplified guitar music. My father parked our car in the grass on the side of the road, and we walked till we reached the crowd.

Once there, we were relieved to see that the attraction was, as we suspected, a guitar duo that went by the stage name *The Cherokee Sweethearts*. We hoped these performers, our kin, might help us find lodging for the night.

The Cherokee Sweethearts were my mother's older sister Helen (who took her middle name *Audrey* as her professional name) and her husband, Louis. At the illuminated performance site stood a teepee, backed by a display of hanging ornamental quilts, and a small stage where Helen and Louis sat and played their guitars.

Familiar strains of "Ghost Riders in the Sky" and "Wildwood Flower," played in a Rockabilly style, continued to draw more tourists. When Helen and Louis broke loose with the energetic "Smoky Mountain Rock," children rushed onto the stage and began fast clogging. I watched in wonder, wishing I had the skill and courage to join the cloggers. How fun it would be to dance so uninhibitedly. But being a bashful girl, I clung to my father's side and watched the carefree children dance, imagining myself boldly joining them.

When Louis spotted us in the audience, his face lit up. Dressed like an Indian chief in tan buckskin trousers, vest, and moccasins and a white shirt and white-feathered headdress, he stood and took the microphone from its stand.

"I'd like to welcome our family who've come here from Marion," he announced and pointed in our direction, his husky voice booming in the balmy air. Helen, wearing a white fringed buckskin skirt and sleeveless top and matching beaded headband and moccasins, grinned shyly as her husband made the announcement. She, too, was surprised and pleased to see us. The audience looked our way and applauded our presence there, and I felt like a celebrity.

Louis was a natural showman. He could play the audience as skillfully as his thick fingers played the guitar. When he told a slightly off-color joke, his audience roared. But the next moment he could grow reverent and speak spiritual words, appealing to the Christian convictions of his admirers. Then he and Helen began a rendition of "How Great Thou Art." Some listeners quietly sang along, and I watched a few wipe tears from their eyes.

But then the mood shifted as they lit into "Cherokee Boogie," a brisk piece that lifted the spirits of the audience. Then the slower "Gypsy Guitar," with its drumbeat rhythm and Indian sound, made everyone suddenly feel a kinship with the Cherokee tribe.

In reality, Helen and Louis were no more Native American than the rest of our family, whose roots were more Scotch-Irish than anything. Louis—a stout man with wavy sandy hair and blue eyes—was mostly concealed by his costume, though his tan skin and rounded facial features might have been suggestive of the Cherokee people. But Helen, on the other hand, could easily pass for a Cherokee with her shapely petite build, shoulder-length black hair, dark brown eyes, and pretty face. My mother has often told a story about the time when Helen and Louis joined a wagon train. Dressed in their Indian costumes, they marched alongside covered wagons and horseback riders. An observer spotted Helen and remarked, "You can tell she's an Indian." I'm sure Helen was flattered that people believed she was actually a Cherokee.

The Cherokee Sweethearts had cut albums and 45s at a recording studio in Greenville, South Carolina, which they sold at their performances in Cherokee and at other musical events where they appeared. The albums *Themes of the Smokies* and *Favorite Tunes* were popular tourist items, featuring tunes such as "John Henry" and "Wabash Cannonball." Helen gave my mother a copy of *Themes of the Smokies*, which she eventually passed along to my brother, and a 45 with the tune "Spanish Guitar Strip" on side one and "Cherokee Boogie" on the flip side. I have seen several of Helen and Louis' KLUB label 45s still available on eBay.

Helen, according to my mother, had always played the guitar and enjoyed performing. In fact, she and my mother were a musical duo in the 1930s when they were girls.

"We could sing good," my mother explained. "We harmonized good together. That's all we did—sit on the porch and sing. We sounded as good as anybody on the radio."

"What did you sing?" I asked.

"We sung 'Home on the Range' and Western songs that was popular at the time. We performed at functions," she added. "We sung at a park in Old Fort where people gathered. It was in the newspaper and said 'Music provided by the Davis sisters.'"

"How old were you then?" I asked.

"I was about eleven," she said; "she was thirteen."

A couple of years later, my mother and her sister went to a Spartanburg, South Carolina, radio station to try out for a singing job.

"Helen's boyfriend, Squats, took us," my mother recollected and added he was nicknamed *Squats* because of his short stature.

I asked her if Helen played the guitar for their audition.

"Yes," she said. "I sung 'Shine on Harvest Moon.' We might have sung another one together. I sung melody, and she sung harmony."

She said they must have gotten the radio job because they were asked to come back the following Thursday. But on the drive home to Marion, Helen and Squats stopped along the way and got married.

"If they hadn't got married," my mother lamented, "we'd have had a career in radio."

Helen lost Squats in 1957 to a diabetic coma when he was forty-three. Helen was thirty-six at the time. The following year she married Louis, a World War II Navy veteran who was thirty and a widower.

"How did Helen and Louis meet?" I asked my mother.

"I don't know," she said quickly. "Helen worked out of town at that time, and she no longer lived in Marion."

I always wondered if Helen and Louis met and fell in love because of their mutual guitar playing or if by some chance they met and then discovered their musical kinship. In any case, they must have started making music together professionally soon after their marriage in 1958. In 1963 they won prize ribbons at the Old Time Fiddlers Convention held at Union Grove, North Carolina, and had by then developed a regional reputation.

Hearing them in Cherokee was a thrill for me—the atmosphere was electrifying, and the audience treated them like stars; clearly they were greatly admired there. But I had heard them performing before in a less public circumstance and not as *The Cherokee Sweethearts*.

Occasionally, they would visit us from their home in Drexel, a small town thirty miles east of Marion. Dressed in regular clothes and hauling their guitar cases and amplifier into our house, they set up a performance stage on our front room's hardwood floor. Once they began playing, our neighbors, drawn by the boisterous guitar music, would drop in to listen. Some stood on the front porch and watched the concert through the screen door.

No one complained about the noise, though likely you could hear the amplified music throughout the neighborhood and around the block. The music was vigorous, with its strong percussive rhythms. Heads bobbed, feet tapped, and all the listeners smiled at familiar tunes: some boogie-woogie, some country, and some gospel. Everyone was impressed by Helen and Louis' perfect coordination as they performed together. Though many people in my area at that time could play the guitar—my mother and father included—the virtuosity that my aunt and uncle exhibited was rare.

These home performances were exciting, but seeing my aunt and uncle entertaining at the Cherokee Indian Reservation, dressed in showy costumes as The Cherokee Sweethearts, shed a glamorous light on them. This weekend job was by no means their "day job." Helen worked in a cotton mill in Valdese (having grown up, along with my mother and her other siblings, in Marion's Clinchfield cotton mill village), and Louis worked at the carbon plant in Morganton—a job that his doctor would later associate with Louis' lung cancer, which took his life in 1993. In their town Drexel they lived a normal life, raising her son and his daughter from their previous marriages. Their white frame home with its neat yard adorned by Helen's flowers (which had already begun to bloom that late March in 1998 when Helen died of a heart attack) seemed a source of pride for them. Yet I believe their weekday life was not the one they enjoyed so much as their weekend life spent in the Great Smoky Mountains making music and being deeply appreciated.

That summer evening when my family traveled to Cherokee and could not find a room, we were saved by Helen and Louis. They arranged for us to crash with them and their friends. The accommodations were cramped and dark, and I have little memory of the exact place where we stayed. But my parents were there, so it was all right. We hung close to Helen and Louis the next day and got an insider's view of their weekend world and the people they associated with.

At one of the shops near Helen and Louis' performance site, my father bought me a little red plastic name tag with *JULIA* engraved in white letters. I was touched by this unexpected gift and pinned it to my striped sweater to wear proudly that Saturday. For lunch, my parents and I ate a hot dog, and for dessert I had an ice cream cone from Dairy Queen. My father took me to see the world's smallest horse.

This was one of the last trips we would make to the Cherokee Indian Reservation, and it was the most memorable. My father's endearing gift of the little name tag and the time we spent with The Cherokee Sweethearts made this weekend a special one in my childhood.

II

The Years Flow By

We called ourselves the *Coffee House Writers,* though we mostly met in the conference room of our Marion, North Carolina, public library. Participants of this writers' workshop came and went during our Friday evening meetings. Our leader, Barbara—a charismatic teacher at the county high school and author of two poetry books—provided freshly brewed coffee and a box of pastries or bag of cookies, which seemed to be a great incentive for attendance.

Yet what drew us mainly was a chance to have a responsive audience for our poems and stories. Each week most of us would bring something newly written to read to the group. At the time, I taught English at the local community college and had published short stories and poems in literary journals. Most of the participants, however, were unpublished and untrained professionally. But we were all eager to learn from each other.

As time passed, we settled into a loyal membership: Barbara; Audrey, Barbara's high school student and protégé; Tim, a performer in an experimental rock band; Brent, a laborer; and me.

Always an adventurer and entrepreneur of opportunities and a devotee of Thomas Wolfe, Barbara devised a plan for us to travel to Asheville to hold a photo session at the Thomas Wolfe Memorial and then proceed to Riverside Cemetery for a reading and picnic at Thomas Wolfe's grave. She suggested we wear period clothes, so I searched through dress racks in second-hand boutiques in Black Mountain and found an Edwardian white cotton dress, embellished with lace. I would accessorize with a straw hat.

On a bright spring Sunday afternoon, our group met in Asheville at the Thomas Wolfe Memorial—once known as *Old Kentucky Home*—on North Market Street. The Queen Anne Victorian house, formerly Wolfe's family home and a boardinghouse run by Wolfe's mother, was closed to visitors that day, but we were given permission to take photos on the front porch. We sat in rocking chairs in our antique clothes, pretending we were boarders. (Incidentally, the house would soon be closed for several years because of a fire, set by an arsonist during a street festival.)

After our photo session, we headed to Montford Historic District to find Riverside Cemetery, and Audrey rode with me.

Along the way, I asked her, "Do you know Donovan's music?" Earlier, on the drive to Asheville, I had been listening to his CD collection *Troubadour.*

"No, I don't," she said.

I sensed that Audrey, a talented young poet, was a Romantic at heart. She appreciated classical music and admired the work of Edna St. Vincent Millay. I thought Donovan's lilting voice and the stories he told in his songs might appeal to her.

"Listen to this," I said and selected "Guinevere."

We listened silently as the wistful song played.

When it finished, she said, "That was beautiful."

"I thought you might like it," I said. I told her my husband and I used to listen to Donovan's music on LPs and 8-track tapes in the old days.

Suddenly she said, "You know what we should do?"

"What?" I asked.

"Well, when one of us gets a book published, we should come over here and jump in that fountain downtown to celebrate."

I laughed at the thought. She meant the fountain on Pack Square, a popular spot in downtown Asheville. I could imagine what a scene she and I would make splashing in the water.

"We need to do it," I agreed.

When the group arrived at Riverside Cemetery, we parked our cars near Thomas Wolfe's grave and explored the sprawling tree-shaded grounds. We found O. Henry's gravesite and were surprised by the simplicity of his gravestone that read

WILLIAM SYDNEY PORTER
1862-1910

I thought about his story "The Gift of the Magi," one that was meaningful to me since I had always had long hair like the wife in the story. Every time I read the story, I was moved by the sacrifice she had made getting her hair cut to buy her husband a Christmas gift she couldn't otherwise afford.

Back at Wolfe's grave we all pondered his headstone's elaborate epitaph, which read in part:

TOM

SON OF

W.O. AND JULIA E.

WOLFE

A BELOVED AMERICAN AUTHOR

OCT. 3, 1900-SEPT. 15, 1938

"THE LAST VOYAGE, THE LONGEST, THE BEST"

Barbara had suggested that we pick favorite Wolfe poems or novel excerpts to read, and I chose a passage from his novel *You Can't Go Home Again* that addressed the powerful pull of home and time's fleeting nature.

After our reading, we ate fried chicken, drank sweet iced tea, and enjoyed each other's company in a place that Barbara must have considered sacred. We all hoped that Thomas Wolfe, in his way, knew we were there to honor him.

Barbara also tried to provide publishing opportunities for us, editing a chapbook *Under Court House Hill*, which featured our work and that of her high school students and members of the community. To celebrate the release of this book, the contributors gave a public performance, proclaimed on a printed program as *An Evening of Poetry and Music*. The event was held in the Parish House of St. John's Episcopal Church, where Barbara and I attended. As promised by the program, we read poetry, and Audrey and I provided musical entertainment, I playing the piano and Audrey the flute in a soulful rendering of Satie's *Three Gymnopedies*. Afterwards, refreshments were served: cheese, homemade French bread, finger sandwiches, chips and dip, and fruit punch served from an antique crystal bowl. The evening was a cultural success, well-attended by family and friends, yet Barbara told me the following Sunday, as we sat together at the Parish House during Coffee Hour, that the church's crystal punchbowl had been chipped during the event. This was not good news, as this bowl had been in the church's possession for years, no doubt donated in the past by an esteemed parishioner. A member of the ECW informed Barbara of the catastrophe.

"Was she sure the chip wasn't there before?" I asked in a low voice.

"Yes," Barbara said.

Barbara and I were penitent, both realizing how valuable and irreplaceable the punchbowl was. We discussed how we might compensate the church for the damage. Thankfully, though, nothing more was said to us about the incident, and our writers' group was absolved.

Barbara also encouraged us to go out of our small community to share our creative work, so on a Wednesday evening, several of us piled into my RAV4 and drove thirty miles to downtown Asheville for Malaprop's Bookstore's open mike night. It was a rainy evening, and after we found a parking space in a nearby parking garage, we headed to the bookstore. We had arrived early, so we decided to take a quick tour of the area and found ourselves at the Basilica of Saint Lawrence, a majestic Spanish Baroque Roman Catholic church. We left our umbrellas outside and entered the sanctuary, awed by the magnificent domed ceiling and lovely stained glass windows that depicted scenes from the Scriptures. But we were most touched by the splendidly carved wooden crucifix above the high altar. I think we all felt humbled by the church's grandeur and moved by the spirit we felt there. We lit candles, said silent prayers, and slipped out quietly.

At Malaprop's, a bookstore and café on Haywood Street, we sat at small tables and drank coffee and hot chocolate. While we waited for open mike to be announced, Barbara chatted with store patrons, making friends on the spot. We were all excited, though nervous, to see so many people gathering in the chairs set up in front of the podium.

As we read, Barbara took pictures of us, and later we took group shots in the dingy parking garage. We were pleased with how our readings had gone, happy to be in a big city together, and wanted to remember the evening and everything about it.

The final adventure of the Coffee House Writers was, again, Thomas Wolfe-related. This time Barbara suggested that we meet at Old Fort Cemetery in Old Fort, a township west of Marion.

This was my first visit to Old Fort Cemetery, and only Barbara, Brent, and I were able to meet on this Friday evening. When we arrived at the cemetery, we quickly found what Barbara had wanted us to see: an exquisite marble angel holding a bouquet of withered flowers, her head lowered in mourning. Apparently this Italian sculpture had once been owned by Thomas Wolfe's father, a stone cutter and proprietor of an Asheville monument shop. But he lost the angel in a poker game to a man who would place it at his wife's grave in Old Fort. The sculpture was similar to one described in Thomas Wolfe's novel *Look Homeward, Angel* and was a treasure in Old Fort that most people in our county had never seen.

We admired the angel for a while and then turned to our poems and stories. A man, whom we assumed to be the cemetery caretaker, made his presence known, but he didn't disturb us or ask us to leave. After we finished reading, we talked about our creative lives and our dreams for the future.

"Writing is a comfort to me," I admitted. "I don't know how I'd get by without it."

Barbara and Brent nodded in agreement, and there was an unspoken understanding that being together this way to share our thoughts was a comfort, too. We lingered at the cemetery until dusk.

Soon afterwards, the Coffee House Writers dissolved. Life had gotten in the way.

When Barbara reached retirement age, she moved into an apartment in the Battery Park Hotel in downtown Asheville. Built in 1924, this hotel was listed on the National Register of Historic Places and had been converted into affordable housing apartments for senior citizens. Barbara must have been drawn to the fourteen-story brick-and-limestone hotel because of its architectural beauty and grand history, including visits from Thomas Wolfe and F. Scott Fitzgerald. Audrey left home for the university in Asheville. Tim stayed busy performing gigs with his band, and Brent tragically lost his life in a mobile home fire. In late 1999, my husband and I became parents for the first time in our forties, so my focus shifted from writing to caring for our daughter.

That was over two decades ago, and the years since then have flowed by like water, as Thomas Wolfe would say. But I remember those times, when the Coffee House Writers especially needed each other's company, and I am grateful for what we had then.

Away in a Manger

It was Christmastime in 2001. I had recently resigned my position as organist at St. John's Episcopal Church, but still played for choir practice and now sang soprano in the choir.

Our choir was a small group, and our director suggested we go caroling at a local nursing home. The children of the choir members had made gift bags for the residents and accompanied us that evening. My three-year-old daughter, Annie, was one of these children.

When we entered the nursing home, it was quiet and dimly lit. The lobby featured colorful wallpaper and coordinated window toppers and stylish upholstered couches and chairs. No one sat at the receptionist's desk, but soon we were greeted by a staff member who said she would guide us through the facility and told us we could sing to residents who were awake. As we walked down the hallway, I noticed the cheerful floral prints displayed on the walls.

"This reminds me of a hotel," I told someone in our group, and I thought to myself, *If a person had to live in a rest home, this place wouldn't be so bad.*

As we came to rooms where the occupants were awake, we sang familiar carols like "O Come, All Ye Faithful," "Silent Night," and "Joy to the World." One of our choir members, Lisa, accompanied us on her guitar.

Many doors were decorated with festive wreaths or sparkling silver bells. On some bedside tables stood miniature Christmas trees, adorned with garland and ornaments. Christmas cards were pinned to bulletin boards.

One of the doors was slightly ajar, and on it was tagged the name of my husband's grandfather. Earlier, before Annie and I left home, Steve had told me to be sure to look in on his papaw, who was an Alzheimer's patient at the nursing home.

Annie and I stepped into his room, but saw that he was asleep.

I told Annie he was her great-grandfather. Of course she had seen pictures of him and had heard stories about his service in World War II, but was too young to really know who he was.

"See your picture on his bulletin board?" I said and pointed to it. She nodded, and we stood there quietly for a minute.

"Well, we better go now," I said, and Annie placed a gift bag on his bedside table.

We rejoined our group and continued strolling down the hallways. We came to a room where a woman sat beside the bed of an elderly woman who appeared to be sleeping. We started to pass by this room, but the woman sitting there said, "Would you sing something for my mama?"

"Of course," our director said and asked if she had a particular carol she'd like to hear.

"Could you sing 'Away in a Manger'?" she said. "It's always been Mama's favorite."

As Lisa strummed, we softly sang the carol we all knew well. I remembered singing it as a child in my Baptist church, especially during Christmas plays, and recalled its being the first tune I picked out on a neighbor's upright piano when I was six or seven.

When we finished the carol, the daughter wiped her eyes and said, "Thank you so much for singing that song. I know Mama heard it." And in a low voice she confided that her mama wasn't expected to live till morning. All of us in the choir realized what a sad circumstance we were witnessing.

Only later would I fully appreciate what that daughter must have felt as she sat with her dying mama. My father spent the last year of his life in this same nursing home, and during that time, I visited him daily. I saw the loneliness and confusion of many residents and shared the melancholy and dread felt by other family members who came to visit their loved ones. This was not a hotel. The unsettling sights, sounds, and smells of illness and mental decline were all around. And despite the efforts of nursing home staff and family members to make the residents feel at home—through upbeat social activities and homey room decorations—this place was not home. Death was never far away.

Still, there were moments of solace here, too, such as a daughter and, I hope, her mama found twenty years ago, when my church choir came caroling.

Copperheads

If you grew up in Western North Carolina, as I did, you probably have snake stories to tell.

One of my memories from my childhood in McDowell County involves a summer day when I was riding my horse, Thunder, through my front yard. We came to the cement walk that ran from my house to the street, and I happened to look down to see a copperhead stretched near us. Thankfully, Thunder hadn't noticed the snake. I knew that Thunder, a skittish young horse, would likely spook and run wild with me if he saw the snake, so I tugged his rein and turned him, clicking my tongue and nudging his sides with my heels. We cantered safely to the backyard corral. After I dismounted, I hurried to find my neighbor Neal—an older man and outdoorsman—to tell him about the snake. He came down to my yard with his hoe and promptly severed the snake's head. As was his custom, he hung the snake's body in his garden to ward off crows.

Neal's response to the copperhead was not unusual. I have read that the copperhead can be considered the most dangerous snake in North Carolina because of its presence in many areas of the state, the predominance of its encounters with people, and the fact that most venomous snakebites in North Carolina are received from copperheads. So the copperhead usually elicits concern, especially in those who live in rural areas and spend time outdoors. Many people can relate a story about a family member or acquaintance who has been bitten by a copperhead. The snakebite victim likely suffered pain, swelling, and possible tissue damage in the bite area. I believe some people fear losing a body part, such as a hand or foot, from a copperhead bite. While death from a copperhead bite is rare, the fear of this snake's bite is powerful. It causes most of us to tread carefully in yards or pastures with high grass and in woods, where a snake might be hard to detect.

My husband, Steve, who also grew up in McDowell County, recalls a copperhead story involving his grandmother, who lived in Hankins, a woodsy community near Lake James.

"Granny was down on her knees, pulling weeds around her flowers and bushes," he relates. "She would throw the weeds behind her. Mama was picking up the weeds and throwing them off the bank. Granny threw a handful of weeds, and there was a little copperhead snake in it. Mama started to pick up the weeds and saw the snake.

"'Lord, Mama,' she said, 'you've done picked up a copperhead.'

"Granny turned around, looked and saw it, and then she said, 'Well, kill it.' And then she went back to pulling weeds."

My husband's grandmother was of tough stock and took her hardscrabble life and the presence of copperheads in stride.

But I am not so casual in my reaction to copperheads. Recently, on a June evening at dusk, my husband and I were watching television in our living room. Suddenly, we heard our border collie, Bandit, barking outside. His bark was high-pitched and frantic. We'd heard this tone before and feared that he had come upon a snake. In 2015, he had confronted a large copperhead and was bitten on his face.

I stepped out onto our front porch and looked to see Bandit cornering a coiled snake on our cement driveway, close to our house. I ran back into the house for a flashlight, and when I shined the beam on the snake, I saw that it was light brown with chestnut brown hourglass-shaped bands.

"It's a copperhead!" I yelled to Steve, who came out of the house in his socks and stepped off the porch onto the driveway.

"Don't get too close!" I warned him.

The snake struck Bandit, who grabbed it and shook it furiously.

"Bandit, don't!" I screamed.

Just then, Bandit flung it across the driveway, and it landed near Steve's feet.

"Watch out! Don't let it bite you!" I cried. At that moment, Bandit grabbed the snake and ran with it to the yard.

"No, Bandit!" I screamed, knowing he had already been bitten by this snake and would likely get bitten again.

Steve went inside the house to get his revolver, and I stepped into the yard, keeping the flashlight aimed at Bandit and the snake.

"Try to get Bandit away from the snake," Steve yelled when he came back outside, and I called Bandit, who amazingly dropped the snake and came to me. I held his collar and continued shining the light on the snake, so Steve could see it clearly to get a precise shot. His foremost reason for taking this action was our family's health and safety. He knew if the snake escaped, it would likely come back to our driveway, posing a danger not only for our dog, but also for me, our daughter, or him if one of us got out of our vehicle and stepped on it.

Once again, Bandit survived his snake ordeal. But since that recent June evening, my family has been more vigilant about walking on our driveway from dusk to dawn.

The copperhead is not one of North Carolina's eight snake species protected under the state's endangered wildlife law. So it is not illegal to kill one. Yet I believe most people do not seek out copperheads to destroy. We simply try to avoid them and hope our paths don't cross.

For forty years, my husband and I have lived in the western region of McDowell County, in the neighborhood where he grew up. This is a mountainous area approximately a quarter of a mile from the Pisgah National Forest boundary.

Black bears, foxes, coyotes, deer, raccoons, 'possums, rabbits, and various rodents, amphibians, reptiles, and birds have shared our property.

We have enjoyed our co-existence with these many creatures. Such proximity to wildlife is one of the beauties of living in Western North Carolina. However, with some of these creatures, including copperhead snakes, we prefer to keep our distance.

Our Garden Snake

On an Asheville television news program, a herpetologist explained that September was the time for baby black rat snakes to hatch from their leathery eggs. He brought a mother snake and her hatchlings with him to the studio. He invited the anchors to hold the baby snakes, which he explained were harmless, but noted that they might raise their heads and hiss if they felt threatened.

Living with my family in a rural Western North Carolina neighborhood, I have seen my share of black snakes through the years.

At our first home—a rustic wood-and-stone house—we occasionally had black snakes visit us. One day I headed down the long flight of wooden stairs to the basement laundry area. Reaching the bottom of the stairs, I looked back up, and to my dismay I saw a black snake stretched across the top step. Apparently I had managed to step over the snake without touching it. I could imagine my horror if I had felt the snake under my foot, which would have caused me to tumble headlong to the cement floor below.

In our upstairs bedroom in a storage closet under the rafters of the roof, I once found a dry snake skin that had been shed at some time.

And we had a snake that stayed for a while at the base of our stone chimney. At my request, my husband, Steve, carried it into the woods to relocate it. But it soon found its way back, and we left it alone. It was likely the one that I spied on the basement step and the one that had shed its skin in the attic closet.

Destroying a black snake was not an option to my husband. He had emphasized to me and our daughter, Annie, that we should tolerate black snakes—a nonvenomous species—and not harm them. When I asked him why he especially liked black snakes, he said, "My knowledge of black snakes goes back to my grandfather when I helped him in the garden during the summers."

"Papaw always thought highly of black snakes," he explained. "He had neighbors who had a pig lot, and rats were bad to be around livestock. But black snakes normally kept those rats run off Papaw's property, and a black snake in a garden would scare crows and eat cut worms."

In time, my family moved up the road into my husband's childhood home, and in a corner of the back pasture we raised a garden. While I picked green beans, I regularly saw a black snake—one that we nicknamed *Blackie*—stretched under the bean vines. We came to think of Blackie as our garden snake. I was careful not to step on him, but I wasn't afraid. He seemed to take no notice of me while I worked. And I remembered my husband's words about the benefit of a black snake in a garden.

One day Blackie ventured down through the pasture to the edge of our backyard, where Annie and I noticed him crawling under a chain link gate that lay in the grass. I warned Annie to keep her distance from him—after all, black snakes would bite. But she and I enjoyed watching Blackie slither through the wires of the gate, and I got the camera and took pictures of him.

I hoped Blackie would not come into our backyard. Though tolerant of his presence in the garden and the pasture, I didn't want him near our house.

But as far as I know, Blackie never entered the yard. And in any case, he eventually disappeared, no longer keeping me company in the garden. We suspected that a neighbor caught Blackie in his henhouse and shot him. My husband said that a lot of people who had chickens didn't like black snakes because they ate eggs. "But," he added, "a rat will do more damage to chickens, eating their eggs and chicks, than a black snake will do."

Through the years, there's never been another snake like Blackie that we've grown accustomed to and given a name. But come September, another such snake may hatch and find its way to us.

Watching Crows

Growing up, I saw plenty of crows, but I didn't give them much thought. They were just part of the rural Western North Carolina landscape. Marrying a crow hunter, however, made me more aware of them. My husband, Steve, began hunting crows as a teenager, and after we married, he continued crow hunting in the cornfields along the Catawba River, carrying his Ithaca 12 gauge shotgun.

He's told me he especially enjoyed hunting in fall because of the season's colors and crisp air, when "it was cool enough to wear a flannel shirt and a jacket and be comfortable." I think being outdoors was what he most enjoyed about hunting.

I became better acquainted with crows when Steve and I started planting a garden each spring in our back pasture. A large part of our garden was a corn crop, which attracted crows.

Steve had heard if you hang a dead crow in your garden, other crows would stay away, perceiving the area as unsafe. We tried this one year, and it helped deter crows from damaging our corn crop. Ordinarily, though, we made a scarecrow and placed it at the head of the corn patch. We also stretched strings with aluminum pans attached throughout the garden and hung wind chimes on poles at the end of rows. We mounted an owl decoy on a fence post as a sentinel. Despite these preventative efforts, the crows still came and did their damage.

Obviously, a crow is a smart bird, not easily duped. Indeed, the crow has been hailed as the most intelligent bird in North America. Steve has always attested to a crow's intelligence, explaining to me that crows have a unique language that features different calls with a varied number of caws. This language includes fight calls, when an owl or hawk is spotted near their nest; feeding calls, when food—an animal carcass or source of grain—is available; and distress calls, when an attack by a predator or a member of an opposing flock occurs. While telling me about these calls, Steve recounted an incident when he and a friend were crow hunting in a fresh-cut cornfield near Lake James.

"There was a flock of crows that flew over. We shot, and I killed one, but my friend hit one and winged it pretty bad. It spiraled down like a maple seed. It gave a distress call, and the other crows that had flown away when we began shooting turned and came back and started flying around the wounded crow. It was enlightening to me to see how protective crows were of each other." I believe this occurrence gave Steve a deeper respect for crows.

We no longer raise a garden. Today my connection with crows is amicable. At daybreak, they fly through the sky and perch in the treetops. Sometimes I hear their *caw! caw! caw!* before I see them. I stand at my kitchen window and watch them as they settle on the grassy knoll across the road from my house. Here they eat scraps I've thrown out—beans, cornbread muffins, oatmeal—my family's leftovers from the evening before or from that morning's breakfast.

My daughter, Annie, teases me about feeding the crows, calling me "The Crow Lady." I tell her, "They're my crow friends," and I find myself waiting for their arrival each day. But the crows are still wary of me. I've wanted to take pictures of them from my front porch, yet they've flown as soon as they saw the front door open. And when I've attempted to take a picture from my kitchen window and accidentally tapped the glass with my camera lens, they scattered. I have managed to get a few distance shots with a zoom lens, but only because I was concealed inside the house. I hope someday the crows will trust me and not fly away when I come near them.

Despite Steve's past as a licensed crow hunter, I can't imagine him harming a feather on a crow's head now. In fact, he encourages me to save scraps for the crows and enjoys watching them as much as I do.

I have named the crows who visit us. Two of them are *Heckle* and *Jeckle,* inspired by the cartoon magpies. Heckle is the largest of our crows, who arrives first and leaves last. He toddles up and down the road, as if he prefers walking to flying.

It's been recorded that crows can live fairly long lives—both in the wild and in captivity—some for decades. They mate for life. Their ability to protect themselves and their fellows through keen senses and effective communication undoubtedly enhances their survival and longevity. According to Carolina Bird Club, the American crow is a common and abundant species in McDowell County, where I live, and its numbers are increasing in the mountain region. So I'm sure Heckle and Jeckle and other such crows will be around for a good while.

Realistically, in luring crows to our property, I may be creating problems for us if we decide to plant another corn crop. But I'll worry about that later. In the meantime, I will enjoy watching crows gather in the morning to share my family's food.

Scarecrow

I've always liked scarecrows. Something about a lonely figure in tattered clothes at the edge of a cornfield moves me.

My affection for scarecrows was probably influenced by *The Wizard of Oz* and the scarecrow in that story. As a child in the 1960s, I looked forward to an annual television broadcast of the movie. Even though my family had a black-and-white Zenith set and we couldn't perceive the color in Oz, we enjoyed watching the movie together.

My mother has often told me about first seeing the movie when she and my father were dating.

"We went to see *The Wizard of Oz* in 1939," she recalls. "We walked to town and saw it at the Marion Theatre."

So *The Wizard of Oz* is meaningful to both me and my mother. Yet despite its influence, I believe my affection for scarecrows goes deeper than admiring a character in a movie.

Through the years, my husband, Steve, our daughter, Annie, and I have had several scarecrows. But one scarecrow was special. In the summer of 2016, our cornstalks were tall and sprouting golden tassels, and we expected little husks to form soon. We knew as soon as the corn appeared, crows would come too. So it was time for a scarecrow.

"Find some of my old clothes," Steve said, and I gathered a pair of overalls, a brown-checkered flannel shirt, a canvas fedora, and a pair of leather work gloves.

Steve cut two pine saplings and wired them together in the form of a cross. He and I dressed the cross, stuffing the clothes with straw. With the back of an ax, he hammered the vertical stake into the ground. He then formed a head from a straw-stuffed nylon feed sack and tied it to the stake. With a permanent marker, he drew the scarecrow's features—eyes, eyebrows, nose, and mouth—and placed the hat on its head.

We stood back and surveyed the creation.

"He's the best scarecrow we've ever had," I said.

"I reckon so," Steve agreed.

In the past, we had named our scarecrows—usually *Clem*. But this time, we simply called him *Scarecrow*.

I was so proud of Scarecrow that I took pictures of him. When I asked Steve to pose with him, Steve put his arm around the square shoulders. Steve took the camera to get a shot of Scarecrow and me, and I, too, put my arm across Scarecrow's shoulders. It seemed natural to do so.

That day, Scarecrow began his job guarding our corn patch.

And all seemed promising for a bountiful garden.

But one night a terrible rain and wind storm came, and I lay in bed and listened to the rain pounding and the wind whistling. The next morning, I rushed to the back pasture where our garden was planted. Three rows of corn had been flattened to the ground as if a tornado had touched down there. Scarecrow leaned forward, his hat askew. But his dreamy eyes and whimsical smile showed no sign of alarm at what he must have witnessed in the night.

"I don't see how you survived," I told him as I straightened him and repositioned his hat. "You're a tough scarecrow."

But despite Scarecrow's vigilance over our corn patch, the corn was a disaster that year. While in past harvests I had gathered wheelbarrow loads of plump sweet ears to preserve, this year my harvest was meager, the undamaged stalks yielding a few spindly stubs.

At the end of that season, I asked Steve, "Should we pull up Scarecrow in case we want to use him again?"

"No, let's just leave him there," Steve said, as if he imagined Scarecrow would be happier left outside rather than stored in the barn.

That was the last year we raised a full garden in the pasture. Since then, I've settled for a few tomato and pepper plants around the patio.

Sometimes I look out of my upstairs window, and through a tangle of vines and weeds I glimpse the top of a hat. For a moment I think a stranger has stolen onto our property.

But then I realize it's only Scarecrow, still guarding what once had been his corn patch.

Hornets' Nest

My dog, Bandit, and I often walk down our rural road, passing a pasture where cows come to the fence to watch us. Recently I looked up at the winter-white sky and spied a large hornets' nest hanging from a sycamore tree.

I recoiled, seeing it hanging above my head, realizing I had never noticed it before. I knew from past experience that being so close to a hornets' nest could be dangerous.

On a Saturday morning in August 2006, I sat on my front porch in a rocking chair, eating toast and drinking coffee. My husband, Steve, sat in the porch swing. We were talking about my scheduled book signing that afternoon at a bookstore in Forest City.

As I ate my breakfast, a bald-faced hornet made a swoop at me. I swatted frantically as it made several passes at my head.

"It's trying to sting me!" I squealed, and Steve rushed to help swat it away.

But it stung my right cheek just below my eye.

I hurried to the bathroom to take a Benadryl tablet.

"I'll go get some After Bite," Steve said and took off to the local convenience store. My aching cheek began to swell, nearly shutting my eye.

I held a cold compress to my face, wondering how I would honor my commitment to the bookstore.

Around noon I applied makeup to conceal the redness. The swelling was still apparent, but the Benadryl and After Bite had helped, and I could see well enough to drive. I didn't cancel the book signing but was embarrassed about my altered appearance.

I located the nest of the hornet that had stung me, hidden in an azalea bush beside our driveway. Steve destroyed the nest, and eventually we cut down the azalea bush.

This incident was slight compared to something that would happen four years later. On a September day in 2010, our daughter, Annie, found a dead hummingbird under the maple tree in our front yard. It had come to drink nectar at the feeder that hung from a tree limb and was attacked by a European hornet. We had noticed these large brown-and-yellow hornets buzzing around the feeder, stealing nectar and attacking hummingbirds.

Angered by the hummingbird's death, Steve watched for hornets at the feeder, and when he saw one, he went and swatted at it.

"Be careful," I warned, and just then I saw him jerk his hand back.

"Did it sting you?" I asked and ran to him. I found a tiny red spot on his wrist bone.

"I think it just glanced off me," he said.

I told him to come in the house.

"Where's your Epi-Pen?" I asked, referring to a self-injectable dose of epinephrine previously prescribed to him when he had an allergic reaction to bee stings.

I found his Epi-Pen in the bathroom and took it to the living room, where he lay on the couch.

I noticed some puffiness under his eyes. "We better use the Epi-Pen," I said.

"The medicine in it looks cloudy," he said. "I think it's expired. I feel okay, just nervous," he assured me.

But his face looked pale, his forehead felt cool and clammy, and he was swallowing peculiarly. Soon he was in the bathroom vomiting.

"I'm calling EMS!" I cried.

The emergency workers arrived and rushed him to the hospital. Thankfully, he recovered, and I took down the hummingbird feeder. I knew our hummingbirds could find nectar in flowers I had planted.

When I recently spied the hornets' nest hanging from the sycamore tree, I wondered how many such nests were around.

I looked for other nests and discovered two more. One was located near the road in a tangle of limbs behind the cow fence. Bandit and I had frequently passed by this nest in warm months, not realizing it was there because of the cover of leaves. It was a thousand wonders we weren't stung.

I studied this abandoned nest and marveled at its intricate paper layers and dark entry hole. Strange how something so forbidding in one season could be fascinating in another.

Yet nature is an enigma. I just hope there won't be any hidden surprises in the months to come.

The Christmas Hawk

Even as a boy, my husband, Steve, loved hawks. Sharp-shinned hawks, Cooper's hawks, red-tailed hawks—he admired them all and saw them often in the woods near his McDowell County home. To some people in Western North Carolina, hawks are perceived as a menace, especially threatening to chickens. But Steve always saw hawks as creatures of beauty, speed, and agility.

He first realized that he wanted a hawk in the early 1960s when he saw an episode of *Walt Disney's Wonderful World of Color* that featured a wildlife story about a couple who trained hawks and were hunting with them on the Plains.

"I looked up *falconry* in *Compton's Encyclopedia,*" he tells me, "and they had a good article on how you went about training a hawk."

As a boy, he spent a lot of time in the woods, and one day when he was walking with his dogs, a hawk flew across the trail and lit in a tree. He and the hawk stared at each other for a few seconds.

"I instinctively raised my hand and whistled," he recalls. The hawk looked at him quizzically, bobbed its head, and flew deeper into the woods. This moment had an indelible effect on him.

As an adult, he grew more interested in birds of prey and knew he wanted to become a licensed falconer. He learned that he would need to find a licensed, established falconer who had a general or master's license to serve as his sponsor, in case he had questions or needed assistance. And he would have to study the laws and guidelines regarding keeping a hawk.

Our fall vacation in 2006 to Sunset Beach on the North Carolina coast began with a stop in Raleigh at the North Carolina Wildlife Resources Commission office. Our eight-year-old daughter, Annie, a third grader then, had received permission to miss school that day, and while Steve took a 100-question examination for his falconer's license, Annie and I sat in a hallway and worked on her school assignments. Steve passed the exam with a grade of 98%, so the next step would be building a mew to house his future hawk.

We had an ample horse barn in a large field behind our house, and Steve had the back side of this barn expanded to accommodate a hawk. Barred windows, perches, and a screened-in weathering area were added. An inspector with the U.S. Fish and Wildlife Service came to measure and inspect the mew. The mew was approved, so Steve could proceed in acquiring a hawk.

He wanted a red-tailed hawk and had been looking for one. His search was over on December 24—Christmas Eve—when a telephone call came from a falconer in our neighboring Buncombe County. This falconer had himself received a call from a local farmer who had discovered a red-tailed hawk whose foot had gotten hung in chicken wire while it tried to get to his chickens.

This falconer had seen Steve's name listed in a registry of the North Carolina Falconer's Association, and since McDowell County wasn't far from Buncombe County, the falconer asked if Steve would like to have the hawk.

"Yeah," Steve said without hesitation. Excited about the news, he called me at my mother's house, where I was busy getting ready for our Christmas Eve celebration there later in the evening.

I put my Christmas preparations aside for the moment, and Steve, Annie, my mother, and I piled into my Jeep and headed to Black Mountain to meet the falconer and pick up the red-tailed hawk. We met him in a parking lot and transferred the cardboard box that held the hawk, taped up to keep it from moving and injuring itself, from his vehicle to mine.

This being Christmas Eve, Steve thought of St. Nicholas and thus named the female hawk *Nikita*, whom we quickly began to call *Nikki*.

Nikki was a first year bird, around five months old, and when Steve brought her home, he began the process of "manning" her—a necessary first step to get the hawk used to being around him to lose its fear. On the first day, he sat with her for a couple of hours. The next day he sat with her for four hours. On that second day—Christmas Day—she began to feed. As part of her training, he would offer her small bits of meat—beef heart or chicken liver—until she looked at him as a food source. Soon she began feeding on his gloved fist. In time, he moved back away from her to make her fly to him, and within about two weeks, she began free-flying outside.

"She was an easy bird to train," he now reflects.

Admittedly, I was afraid of Nikki and warned Annie not to get close to her. I kept my distance, too.

Nikki was a moderately large hawk who had an intense golden glare, a hooked beak, and sharp talons. Though my husband wore a leather gauntlet when he held her on his fist, I worried about his safety. But he had bonded with her and seemed to trust her as she trusted him.

Yet Nikki could be willful, and one day she got herself into trouble.

Steve had her on his fist in our back field when she saw something, jumped off his glove, and jerked the leash, connected to her leather ankle jesses, out of his hand. She flew and lit in a poplar tree, getting her leash hung in a limb.

"I had to untangle her with a long stick," Steve recalls.

"And then she came back down to you," I say, recalling the incident and remembering how relieved we were when she came to his whistle.

Another unsettling situation with Nikki occurred when Steve was free-flying her in the field.

"I released her, and she flew about a hundred yards and lit in a tree," Steve recalls. "I waited around for a little while to see if she spotted any game. Then after a while, I raised my fist and whistled. She started to fly back and suddenly closed her wings and hit the ground in the high grass. I could see that there was some commotion going on. I walked up there and discovered that she had captured a big snake, and she was in the midst of clawing and pecking it, and it was striking at her, trying to defend itself. I must admit that trying to take an angry snake from a mad hawk is pretty scary."

"What kind of snake was it?" I ask.

"It was a large water snake," he says. "A water snake looks a lot like a copperhead," he adds, so I know that he must have feared she was tangling with a poisonous reptile.

Steve kept Nikki for a little over two years. He has told me that a female red-tailed hawk reaches its sexual maturity at two years old, and then it gets testy and independent.

"Their natural instinct to nest and raise little hawks kicks in," he explains.

This instinct, along with other circumstances, affected Nikki, and Steve remembers the day when everything changed between him and his hawk.

"She'd been free-lofted—flying inside the mew without being tethered—for a week while we were on vacation," he says. "And I fed her a lot before we left because I knew I wouldn't be able to feed her for a week. When we got back from vacation, I noticed that one of her jesses was worn and about to come apart. So I was changing the jess, and she pitched a fit and clawed me pretty bad on the right wrist. An overweight bird can be difficult to handle. So I decided to hack her back to the wild—slowly introduce her to the natural environment—because I realized then that she wanted to go and find a mate."

Indeed, she had clawed him badly, and his wrist became inflamed and swollen. I took him to the doctor, who treated the infected wound with a tetanus shot and antibiotics.

Steve understood why she attacked him and has never held any ill will against her nor been discouraged from wanting another hawk someday.

"If you had your wish," I ask, "what type of hawk would you most want to train?"

"A Cooper's hawk," he says, "or a male red-tailed." I know from conversations with him through the years, especially while we've hiked in the woods and seen hawks flying overhead, that he's always aspired to train a Cooper's hawk. I hope someday that wish will come true.

While Nikki was my husband's hawk, I observed the hard work that he invested in her. I also realized how much a part of our family she became for those two years. I know he missed her after he released her, and we all—Steve, Annie, and

I—looked up to the sky when we heard the familiar red-tailed hawk's cry, thinking Nikki might have come home again. Though it's been over a decade since Nikki flew away from us, I still look up when I hear that distinctive sound.

A falconer's connection with his or her hawk is like no other relationship, and I'm glad I was witness to such a connection.

Those Golden Years

Mountains surround the McDowell County home that my husband, Steve, and I share with our daughter, Annie. The woods are dense with oaks, poplars, dogwoods, and pines, and the air is pungent with the scent of galax. Evening comes early here in the shadows of the trees, and even on summer days, the breeze off the creek in front of our house is cool.

As a boy, Steve lived in the shadows of these same woods, and he explored the rugged trails on foot or motorcycle.

According to Steve, his interest in motorcycle riding was stirred by "watching that movie *The Great Escape*." In fact, in our house Steve displays a framed poster depicting a scene from the film—Steve McQueen sitting on his motorcycle, which Steve explains is "a Triumph modified to look like a German World War II-era BMW."

Around the age of ten when Steve first saw *The Great Escape,* he also acquired his first motorcycle.

"It was a three-horsepower minibike that came from a local auto parts place" he tells me. "It had a Lawson engine." He enjoyed riding this minibike in the woods around his house.

As a teenager, Steve honed his riding skills at an abandoned gravel pit near the Catawba River—a large field with mounds of gravel and sand. He, his friends, and a few older riders congregated there to test their abilities.

"It was like our desert course," he reminisces. At the time, he admired Southern California desert racers like Lee Marvin, Keenan Wynn, and Steve McQueen, celebrities he read about monthly in *Cycle World Magazine.*

"We'd do wheelies and jump over piles of sand. When it snowed, we really had a ball because we'd ride in the snow, power sliding. When we got wet, we'd go to Gibson's General Store to sit by the potbelly stove, eat cheese crackers and drink coffee, and dry out. Then we'd go back and ride again."

During this same time, Steve became a competitive rider.

"I raced motocross at Steele Creek on the North/South Carolina border," he explains. "I was sponsored by Yamaha of Asheville and raced in the 250 class. I rode a 1970 Yamaha 250 MX."

A trophy now stands on a shelf in a storage room at our house, attesting to his skill at motocross racing.

"I also ran several flat dirt track races at the I-26 Raceway near Hendersonville on a 1968 Triumph TR5. This track was faster than motocross."

In his late teens, Steve participated in motorcycle trials in Gainesville, Georgia. Here he maneuvered his Honda Trials 125 through the woodsy obstacle course, crossing logs and rocks, trying not to set his feet down as he confronted these traps.

"That was the end of my motorcycle competitive life," he reflects. "I didn't have the time."

Yet he continued to enjoy motorcycle riding.

What he especially liked about woods riding was "constantly seeing wildlife, seeing what was around the next ridge, and clearing trails."

He also enjoyed riding "some of the bad places" in the county, such as the Narrow Knob.

He explains that "the Narrow Knob was a very difficult old fire trail that joined Mackey's Creek to the head of Curtis Creek Road. The fire service kept it maintained in case they had to go in there and fight a forest fire. It ran into the head of Curtis Creek, near the Blue Ridge Parkway. It was a treacherous terrain."

When he tackled this terrain, he rode a small trail bike, such as a Hodaka Ace 100 and later a Yamaha 250 Enduro. But one day he rode a Honda Trials 125 and had a harrowing misadventure.

"I was riding by myself," he says, "and I ran off the trail into a very steep rocky and ivy-choked ravine. I had to turn the motor off and drag the bike one end at a time back up to the trail. It took about an hour. I had a few bruises and scratches, but otherwise I wasn't hurt."

He recalls what waited beyond the Narrow Knob.

"One of my favorite places to ride was down through Chestnut Cove. After going through the Narrow Knob, the trail went down into a cool, dark flat. The ground was like potting soil, covered by fern, galax, and other plants that gave off an almost sweet smell. Giant hemlock trees blocked the sun. Lying on the ground were logs of dead chestnut trees, killed by blight many years before. If you took a hatchet and cut beneath the rotten-looking surface, a beautiful golden-brown grain was revealed. This part of the Pisgah National Forest was a bear sanctuary, so my friends and I often saw young bears darting across the trail and up a tree. There were also timber rattlers, and you had to be careful where you set your feet down. Back then we wore knee-high lace-up boots called *linesmen's*. They offered good protection for the feet and lower legs.

"After Chestnut Cove, the trail turned up into the head of Curtis Creek. From there it was a short distance to the Blue Ridge Parkway where we took a snack break before heading back."

Though Steve owned many motorcycles through the years, he says "the most well-balanced, best handling woods bike I ever had was a Spanish-built Montesa King Scorpion. It had a red fiberglass tank and a chrome-plated frame."

He rode this motorcycle when he performed stunts, some that had unexpected rewards.

"I have a fond memory of the Jumbo Grill," he reminisces, noting a 1950s-style diner in Marion that I too recall from my childhood and teenage years. "It was run by a large man Ed Hester or *Big Ed*, as we called him. Big Ed was fascinated by our dirt bikes and always welcomed us and was happy that we made his joint our headquarters. Back then, you could ride a stripped-down dirt bike on the road if you tagged it for daylight use only.

"Big Ed would often get me to do wheelies, standing on the seat, in the parking lot. One day he was sitting in his booth talking with a friend, and I could tell he was talking about me. I heard the other man say, 'No way. I'd love to see that.' Big Ed said, 'Hey, Duncan, do me a wheelie in the parking lot.' I went outside, fired up the Montesa, and made a few laps around the lot and then sat it back down. When I went back inside, on the table in my booth were a complimentary burger, fries, and Coke. The Jumbo Grill made the best burgers in the county with slaw, chili, mustard, and onions on a soft steamed bun. We all practically lived on them."

Steve's most recent motorcycle was a Triumph Bonneville, a replica of the 1968 model, which he occasionally rode on the congested highways near our home. A few near-accidents caused by negligent drivers spooked him, but a couple of years ago he decided to sell the Triumph to help buy Annie her first car. The sacrifice was bittersweet.

Today as we sit on our front porch, Steve looks across the road at the woods.

"I would like to be able to ride in the woods again," he tells me. "I often think back on those golden years of good friends, blue skies, colorful autumn leaves, and a cool nip in the air. No better time could young men have."

I, too, hope he has the chance to ride those familiar trails again.

The Wampus Kitty

My husband, Steve, has often told me about a mysterious wildcat that he first heard about and saw in his teens, a creature similar to one found in Western North Carolina folklore.

"There were two men who had spent years in the mountains, hunting and making a beverage from corn, sugar, and yeast," Steve recounted recently. "They told us younger boys about a wildcat they'd seen. It was at least as big as a German shepherd and appeared to have horns growing out of its ears. Its eyes glowed like a campfire. It wasn't known to bother anybody, but remains of animals it had killed were found in the woods, and it was big enough to drag a deer up a tree. They called it the *Wampus Kitty*."

Steve himself spent much of his youth exploring the mountains of McDowell County. On a spring night when he was fifteen, he and three friends started up Mackey's Mountain on their trail bikes. They were headed to a cabin at the peak of the mountain for an overnight stay.

Near the summit of the mountain, they came to a steep red-clay bank, a challenging section of the trail.

"We would go one at a time up the bank so if one had trouble we wouldn't all get jammed up in a rough place," Steve explained. "I went first, and when I got near the top, I saw something in the middle of the trail that I thought was a big rock that had rolled off the ridge. When I got closer and my motorcycle headlight struck the figure, I realized it was an animal. At first I thought it might be a bear, but when it turned to look at me, I saw it was a big cat."

"What did it look like?" I asked.

"It had long tufts of fur coming out of its ears and whiskers jutting out from its jaws. Its eyes glowed reddish-yellow like the base of a wood fire. I was so startled that I let my hand slip off the clutch, killing the engine and making the headlight go out. A few seconds later, Brownie came up the trail behind me, and his headlight hit on the big cat. Close behind Brownie were Eddie and Mike, whose headlights lit up the woods. We all saw the cat before it loped away. I restarted my motor, looked back at the boys on their bikes, and heard one of them yell, 'Let's get out of here!' We knew a cat that size could kill a man. We lit out fast up the mountain and rode hard until we got to the cabin."

Because they had forgotten to get the cabin's key from the owner, they had to sleep on the cabin's porch—what sleep they managed to get.

"We spent the biggest part of the night talking about what we'd seen," Steve said.

The following week at school, Steve and his friends went to the library to research large cats. In a wildlife book, they found a picture of a lynx and decided that was the kind of cat they'd seen. But after talking about their sighting to a wildlife official, they weren't sure.

"Walt, our local wildlife officer, told us there weren't any lynxes in the state of North Carolina," Steve said. "He looked at us with the same disbelief that we had felt when ol' Bill and Charlie told us about the Wampus Kitty. But we knew what we saw."

"Did anybody consider it might have been a bobcat?" I asked.

"We knew it wasn't a bobcat because it was twice the size of any bobcat we'd ever seen. And it couldn't have been a cougar because its body wasn't long enough, and it didn't have a tail."

"So you believe the animal you saw was the Wampus Cat?"

"I know it existed that night."

"Did you ever see it again?" I asked.

"None of us ever saw it again."

Steve's love of exploring the mountains here in McDowell County was not altered by his confrontation in 1970. Yet I'm sure he was more cautious, especially at night, after coming face-to-face with that fiery-eyed cat.

III

Her Wedding Ring

When I was a girl, I became interested in antiques. My fascination with old things was probably sparked by the upstairs bedrooms in my paternal grandmother's house. To reach these bedrooms, you first had to enter the downstairs bedroom where my grandmother slept. Inside this room was a narrow dark staircase. The steps of this staircase were not deep, and even a child's foot barely fit, so you had to be careful of your footing when you climbed these stairs.

By the time I came along, my grandmother's upstairs rooms had been deserted by my father and his brothers, who had once slept there. His sisters had married long before and moved on, too. Now the rooms were quiet places holding treasures from the past. In the darker back bedroom that faced the backyard and creek was a clothesline stretched across the room, on which hung my late grandfather Matthew's suits, along with World War I uniforms that had been worn by my grandmother's younger brothers, Condia and Charlie. To a child, entering this room was like stepping into an old tailor's shop—dark and musty and a bit scary, with the uninhabited suits and uniforms hanging mute with memories.

But in the second, lighter bedroom that faced the front yard and the road were a white cast iron bed with scrollwork and rosettes on the headboard; a trunk of souvenirs, which included the Purple Hearts awarded to my uncles who were injured in World War II; and a Victorian photograph album that held tintypes, carte de visites, and cabinet cards of my grandmother's family back in Newcomb, Tennessee. Standing against a wall was a bookcase brimming with school books once used by my father and his siblings—geography, mathematics, and literature texts—and religious books that explicated and promoted the Baptist faith, attesting to my grandfather's calling as a Baptist preacher. Two large framed portraits stood in a corner. The first, in a rectangular gilt-edged oak frame with antique glass, was an early portrait of my grandfather. A handsome young man with neatly parted dark hair, he wore a black dress coat, a white shirt with a high wing collar, and a bow tie. His expression was shy. The second, in an oval gilded frame with convex glass, was a portrait of my great-grandfather Daniel Lynch, my grandmother's father. Dressed in a drab military uniform, Dan, as he was called, appeared to be middle-aged, and his expression was hard.

Also here upstairs was the oak and cane wheelchair used by my great-grandmother Julia Lynch, Dan's wife, in her later years after she fell and broke her hip.

One day I asked my grandmother if she could give me some items to start my antique collection. She gathered a couple of green Ball Mason jars, a pure aluminum syrup pitcher, and a kitchen gingerbread clock that, according to my mother, once stood on a shelf in the dining room and was wound by my grandfather every night before bed. Having lived in my grandparents' house for two years while my father served as a Merchant Marine in World War II, my mother became close to the family and knew their habits well. Reminiscent of the grandfather's clock in the old song, my grandfather's kitchen clock stopped running after he died. So by the time my grandmother gave it and its key to me in the mid-1960s, it didn't work. But its fancy carved wood and glass door with gold butterfly designs made it a nice addition to my collection.

My grandmother also gave me some items that had belonged to her mother: a pair of spectacles with round lenses stored in a hard case, a shoe button hook, two thimbles, a folding skeleton key, two tunic collar disks from Charlie's WWI uniform, and a gold wedding ring. Thinking about it now, I realize it's odd that she would give me such a precious piece of jewelry that had belonged to her mother. I never considered myself her favorite grandchild, and she had several older granddaughters, but she must have wanted me to have the ring.

Still, at the time, the wedding ring didn't mean much to me. Neither of my parents ever wore a wedding band, so I didn't appreciate the ring's symbolism or have any interest in its monetary value. It was just something old, which was what I wanted.

In later years, however, I began to be curious about the ring and the great-grandmother who had worn it.

A few facts I have learned through the years: Julia Ann Baker Lynch, recorded as *Juley* or *Julie,* respectively, in 1900 and 1910 census reports, was born in 1868 in Jackson, Tennessee. In my grandmother's family photograph album is a tintype of her mother as a young girl. It must have been made around 1880. Her hair is dark, her bangs short, and she wears a dark, wide-brimmed hat. Her white dress contrasts with her hair and hat, and she holds a decorative fan in her left hand. Her face is pretty, though her expression is solemn. The first time I looked at this photograph years ago, I thought she resembled Angela Cartwright, a popular young actress during my childhood.

Other pictures of her in the album show a young woman with a growing family. In one cabinet card, she and her husband, Dan, sit casually in a grassy spot, fallen leaves around them. Neither of them looks at the camera. With them are their toddler, Annie, (my grandmother) and baby son, Condia, both in white gowns.

In this picture, my great-grandmother wears a smart dark dress with a black velvet collar, on which a silver brooch is attached. A line of buttons down the bodice and a wide band around her midriff accentuate her full bust and small waist. She wears earrings, and her dark hair is swept up in the Gibson Girl style of the day. In her right hand she holds a white handkerchief.

In another cabinet card, my great-grandparents sit side by side in straight chairs, trees behind them, and they look directly at the camera. His hair has thinned, and her face and figure have matured. Her skirt and blouse are more homespun in material and design than the dress in the earlier picture, though she still fashionably wears small hoop earrings. I can tell by the way her full lips faintly protrude that she has a slight overbite. I imagine this is something I might have inherited from her, besides my first name (which, incidentally, I also inherited from my mother and her grandmother). Their six children, who also look intently at the camera, appear in the portrait with them: Condia and Charlie stand behind their parents, Annie and Pernia beside their father, and Birdie beside her mother. The toddler, Oma, stands in front, braced between her parents' knees. The two oldest girls, Annie and Birdie, wear their hair up like their mother. My grandmother would continue wearing her hair in this style until her death at eighty-four.

Condia and Charlie would eventually serve in World War I. Six letters, written by my great-grandmother from her home in Pruden, Tennessee, to her older son Condia in France, were preserved among my grandmother's photographs. All these letters, however, were returned to her in June 1919. Most of the envelopes have the message RETURNED TO WRITER and word UNCLAIMED stamped on them. Thus, all Julia Lynch's expressions of love and concern for her sons, Condia and Charlie, went unread at the time.

Though my great-grandmother's letters to Condia were returned to her, Condia had already come home by then, having been honorably discharged April 9, 1919. Charlie would arrive home the next April when he was honorably discharged in 1920.

I can only imagine her anguish during those weeks when she didn't know if either of her sons would come back home to her.

I once asked my father what he remembered about his grandmother. He said, "I was the one who found her after she fell outside. I carried her into the house, and she was heavy."

She had broken her hip. This accident would have happened when she was older and living in the house next door to my grandmother and her family in Marion, North Carolina. My father's cousin Clyde was then living with my great-grandmother—his grandmother—having been orphaned at seven years old in Virginia when his father, Dan, a coal miner, and his mother, Birdie, my grandmother's younger sister, died of tuberculosis.

After her fall and subsequent hip surgery, which according to my father was unsuccessful and "she never walked again," my great-grandmother and Clyde moved in with my grandmother and her family.

"What was she like?" I asked my father.

"She was grouchy," he said, though he clearly cared for her to have rescued her after her fall.

My mother remembers her as being "sweet."

The day my mother met her was also the day she met the rest of my father's family.

"He wanted to take me to meet the family," she recalls.

Though she and my father had already been married for a couple of months, she had continued living at her mama's house. But on that November day in 1939, she went to the house where later she would live during my father's term of enlistment in the Merchant Marines.

On that day—November 5, 1939—my father took her into the front downstairs bedroom where his grandma Lynch lay in bed, very sick. He asked my mother if she would help him reposition his grandma, to make her more comfortable.

"She had white hair, parted in the middle and balled up behind," my mother says, and it occurs to me that, like my grandmother, she must have kept the Gibson Girl hairstyle throughout her life. "She was not a small person," my mother adds, making me recall my father's remark that she was heavy when he carried her into the house. Unlike her daughter, my grandmother, who developed a delicate frame in her later years (and became white-haired at thirty-two), my great-grandmother must have kept the stout build indicated in some of her earlier photographs.

"When we went to turn her over," my mother says, "she looked directly at me and told him, 'She's pretty.' I remember she had on that wedding ring," my mother adds, referring to the one my grandmother gave me. "I slept on the couch that night," she says, explaining that my father stayed upstairs where he and his brothers and cousin Clyde slept. The mohair couch that served as my mother's bed that night was located in the front room, across from my great-grandmother's bedroom.

"She died the next day," my mother says. And though my mother hardly knew the family, much less the neighborhood, my grandmother sent her to get two neighbor women—one who lived up the road and one next door where my great-grandmother had once lived—to come to the house after the death. My mother walked to both houses and brought back the women.

According to my great-grandmother's death certificate, she died at 3:45 p.m. on November 6, 1939, of myocarditis, a heart condition from which she had suffered for a few years. She was seventy-one years old.

Years ago when I was visiting my aunt Carcenia, my father's older sister, I asked her to tell me about her grandma Lynch. Being the oldest of my father's siblings, born in 1912, she vividly remembered the family's years in Newcomb,

Tennessee.

"Well," she said, "I know she couldn't stay with Grandpa Lynch. He was all right till their children grew up, but then he changed. And he got so bad she had to leave him."

By what my aunt told me that day, I concluded that my great-grandfather's personality became so erratic that my great-grandmother felt unsafe living with him. Yet, I was surprised to hear of a rural Tennessee woman in the early twentieth century leaving her husband under any circumstances.

Carcenia must have felt close to her grandma, as she did her mama, whom she took into her care during my grandmother's last illness. She certainly seemed sympathetic to her grandma's marital plight. And her grandma loved her, too, their mutual affection indicated by a comment in one of my great-grandmother's letters to Condia:

pruden tenn
september 23 18

. . . say condia carcenia stayed up hear two weeks and wanted to
stay longer and i missed her when they took her home. . . .

What Carcenia told me about my great-grandmother's marital situation continues to puzzle me. But now since Carcenia has passed on, along with my father and all his other siblings, I have no one left who might have insight into my great-grandmother's life and circumstances.

But I still search for clues in census reports, death certificates, military records, and old photographs.

In the 1920 United States Federal Census for Campbell County, Tennessee, Julia Lynch and her son Charlie are recorded as living in the same household. At this time, Charlie would have recently been discharged from military service. His mother, fifty-two years old, is listed as head of the household in a home she owns. Though she is classified as "married," her husband, Dan, is not indicated as a member of her household.

On Dan Lynch's death certificate, his death having occurred on July 5, 1929, his residence at the time of his death is noted as Pioneer, Tennessee. He is listed as a coal miner, an occupation he shared with his sons, Condia and Charlie, and his cause of death is stated as being "pelegra" (pellagra) and "nervis trubel" (nervous trouble). By my investigations, I have found that pellagra is a disease caused by niacin deficiency and has a symptom of extreme nerve dysfunction. So here, in his death certificate, is a hint about his personality disorder that must have driven my great-grandmother away from him. And yet exactly how his "nervis trubel" manifested itself in his behavior, I will never know. Only my great-grandmother herself carried the memories and emotional scars of his behavior with her to the grave ten years after her husband's death. I imagine he suffered, too, though, perhaps being unable to control his actions, whatever exactly they were.

One action that remains a mystery to me is my great-grandfather's enlistment in the military. I have no proof of his military service other than the portrait that was once stored in my grandmother's upstairs bedroom and now belongs to me. Its gold frame is embellished by raised emblems of American flags and a laurel wreath. The oval portrait is set against a colorful backdrop of a waving American flag, an eagle perched atop the portrait and the letters **USA** beneath.

In the portrait, my great-grandfather wears an olive drab wool tunic and campaign hat exactly like the doughboy uniforms worn by his sons, Condia and Charlie, in their photographs. In searching for information regarding my great-grandfather's military service, I found a headstone application for a military veteran Daniel E. Lynch, who was buried in Pioneer, Tennessee. This document, dated 1931, indicates that Daniel E. Lynch enlisted on September 21, 1919, which would have been less than a year after the Great War's end. My great-grandfather Daniel Elbert Lynch was indeed buried in Pioneer, Tennessee. But he would have been fifty-two in September 1919, and my research tells me that the cut-off age for first-time military enlistees during World War I was forty-five. Another problem is the veteran's death date—1926—recorded on this application. My great-grandfather died in 1929. But I have seen factual errors in documents such as this one, so this inconsistent death date doesn't dissuade me from thinking the veteran referred to in the headstone application could be my great-grandfather.

His late-life enlistment, or possibly reenlistment, would certainly explain why his wife was living with her son Charlie (and not with her husband) in 1920—during Dan's supposed term of service.

My great-grandfather's military portrait is clearly one of a mature man. His face is lined, his eyes hooded, and his expression stern. Whether or not the portrait dates from the World War I era, I can't say for sure. Yet my great-grandfather's own sons' service in World War I might have been his incentive to enlist.

In 1930, a year after Dan Lynch's death, Julia Lynch is listed in a Federal Census report as being a "widow" and a member of the household of her son Condia, himself divorced at the time. According to the document, they reside in Marion, North Carolina. She would continue living in Marion until her death at my grandmother's house and be laid to rest in a local Baptist church cemetery. On her tombstone is inscribed:

JULIA ANN LYNCH

JAN. 4, 1868

NOV. 6, 1939

SHE WAS THE SUNSHINE OF OUR HOME

By what I have learned, my great-grandmother suffered as a parent—worrying about her two sons far away in France during World War I and losing her daughter Birdie in 1935 and her son Condia in 1937 to tuberculosis. And she suffered in her marriage to a husband whose behavior must have bewildered her.

Mercifully, she did not live long enough to see the death of her grandson Condia, Jr., who would have been eight in 1930 when she lived with his family. This boy, like so many in my father's family, would grow up to serve his country in World War II. But unlike my father and his four brothers, their cousin Condia, Jr., would not return home. A year after he enlisted, he was captured while serving in the Philippine Islands. He would die in a Japanese prisoner-of-war camp eight months later in June 1942. He was twenty years old.

Today I hold the wedding ring that my grandmother gave me when I was a girl. At the time, it meant no more than the clock and the other items that she gathered for me. I knew nothing then about the great-grandmother who had once worn the ring.

As I now hold the wide gold band between my forefinger and thumb, I admire its luster and its lightness. When I slip it on my own ring finger, I am amazed how perfectly it fits as if it were sized for me. I stretch out my left hand and study how it looks. I wonder how many times my great-grandmother held her hand before her in the same way, especially in the early years of her marriage. As time passed, she might have forgotten it was even there, it seemed so much a part of her finger.

A wedding ring symbolizes perfect union and devotion. For her that union brought children and grandchildren she dearly loved and who must have brought her great joy.

I try to imagine a day in early November 1889, in a coal mining village in Tennessee, when a pretty dark-haired girl of twenty-one offered her hand to a solemn man of twenty-two, and he slipped a ring on her finger.

In time, though, their union would be marred by fear and separation. But despite that, her wedding ring—a symbol of her marriage—remained on my great-grandmother's finger till her final November day, fifty years later.

Besides her name, certain physical features, and a few possessions, I hope I have also inherited Julia Lynch's attributes of strength and perseverance.

The Stone Cutter's Tools

On a Sunday afternoon in 1970, my father, mother, friend Susie, and I loaded up in our Chrysler and headed to Highway 226. After a drive up the mountain road, we came to the Blue Ridge Parkway.

On the parkway, we rode slowly, taking in hillsides covered in wildflowers and bordered by split-rail fences. When we came to an overlook, my father pulled off and parked so we could get out and see the deep valley and mountain ranges that stretched for miles. The air was cool, and we sat and ate our picnic dinner, feeling we had traveled back in time.

It was a memorable summer drive on the Blue Ridge Parkway and one of several we would take during my girlhood.

When we started back home and passed under a stone bridge, my father said, "My uncle helped build this parkway." He said this often in those days.

As I grew older, I came to understand that his uncle Condia Lynch did indeed help build the Blue Ridge Parkway.

Like others in my father's family, Condia was born in Newcomb, Tennessee, and eventually settled in Marion, North Carolina. In his twenties, he served as a U.S. Army infantryman during World War I, was wounded in action in France, and treated at a base hospital. Upon his military discharge in 1919, he returned home to Tennessee and to his job as a coal miner.

But in the 1930s, after settling in North Carolina, he was employed by the Civilian Conservation Corps—a work relief program created by President Franklin Delano Roosevelt. Sympathetic to World War I veterans, FDR put many of these men, along with others unemployed, to work in the CCC. In Western North Carolina, one of their projects was to help build the Blue Ridge Parkway, which involved landscaping, road and bridge building, and stone masonry.

My mother remembers seeing CCC workers during her girlhood in Marion.

"You'd see them in town on Saturday," she recalls. "You knew they were in the CCC camp because of their uniforms. They dressed like servicemen, and you kind of looked up to them. When we drove up the mountain, you could see them working along the highway. Some of them boys was good-looking."

In photographs made during his World War I days, my great-uncle Condia was attractive. Tall and slender in his doughboy uniform, he posed with his rifle and bayonet and made a striking soldier.

But when he worked in the CCC, he was in his forties and divorced, there being no age or marital status restrictions for veterans. Unlike the single boys my mother remembers—typical CCC enrollees who were between eighteen and twenty-five years old—Condia was a mature man, tempered by war and life, when he worked on the Blue Ridge Parkway.

Of course my father's best memory of the CCC was his uncle Condia's connection with it.

Years ago while I was visiting my parents, my father said he wanted to give me something.

I followed him outside to his tool building. He unlocked the door, and we went inside. On a wooden shelf sat a tattered toolbox.

"This belonged to my uncle," he said and opened the toolbox. He removed several chisels. "My uncle used these stone cutter's tools when he worked on the Blue Ridge Parkway."

"Oh, yes," I said and picked up a chisel, remembering how often he had spoken about his uncle's stone work.

"I want you to have these tools," he said.

"Are you sure?" I asked, surprised he would give them up. He had been a hosiery mill machine fixer for years and treasured his own tools. As a child, I spent Saturday mornings with my parents while they worked in the mill. To pass the time, I played with my father's tools. Perhaps he remembered this.

"Yeah," he confirmed. So with my husband's help, I lugged the toolbox home, honored by the gift.

Today I still have the old toolbox, though I transferred the tools to a newer metal toolbox my father gave me before he died. I felt the tools would be safer in this container.

Occasionally, I open my toolbox to inspect the stone cutter's tools and imagine how Condia might have used them. And now when I drive with my family on the Blue Ridge Parkway, I find myself saying, "My great-uncle helped build this parkway."

My Grandmother's Buttons

In my paternal grandmother's house was an old Singer Sewing Machine, kept in a downstairs bedroom, its lid closed for years.

When my family visited my grandmother on weekends, I often went straight to this cool, dim bedroom and pulled open one of the long narrow sewing machine drawers. Here were stored hundreds of buttons, which I scooped out and piled on the floor. I sat cross-legged in front of the treadle and played with them.

These buttons were remnants of my grandmother's family's past. She had snipped them from old clothes, thinking perhaps she might need them again someday. In her collection were buttons of various sizes, colors, and materials: some as big as fifty-cent pieces and others smaller than dimes; pale pinks and greens and ivories; black plastic ones with ornamental designs and plain shiny metal ones. There were brass buttons with anchor and eagle insignia, which she had likely taken from her sons' military uniforms. Bits of material or thread still clung to some buttons. I wondered what clothes these buttons had once been attached to.

Mixed in with the buttons were a silver thimble, a wooden clothespin, a shoe horn, and a souvenir pocket knife from New York City. This knife featured colorful images of the Empire State Building and the Statue of Liberty. My grandmother herself had never traveled farther than a journey from East Tennessee, where she was born and raised, to Western North Carolina, where she, her husband, and their young family settled in the 1920s.

Though I often played with these buttons, I never tired of sifting my fingers through them and trying to find matching sets. Every time I played with them, I discovered new ones I hadn't noticed before.

When my grandmother died and the family distributed her possessions, my mother acquired the sewing machine. She remembered it fondly from the 1940s when she lived with my father's family while he served in the Merchant Marines during World War II.

"I used to sew on that machine," she told me.

She also recalled an outfit my grandmother sewed for her at the time.

"She made me an outfit just like I was her daughter," my mother said. She was always proud of how well she got along with my father's parents and siblings.

Eventually, my mother decided to give the sewing machine to my brother Butch's wife, who liked to sew. Before Butch moved the machine to his house, I asked my mother, "Can I have the buttons?" They were still stored in the same drawer where they'd always been.

"Yeah," she said. "You can go ahead and get them." She knew how much they'd always meant to me.

"I will," I said and didn't waste time doing so.

Today the buttons are boxed and stored in one of my bedrooms. Occasionally I get them out and pour them on the bed, scooping them up in my hands and sifting them through my fingers, still as fascinated by them as ever.

My grandmother's buttons take me back to my 1960s childhood and a cool, dim room where treasures waited in an old sewing machine drawer. I'm grateful I have the buttons to remind me of this time and place.

My Uncle Paul

I remember my uncle Paul—my father's oldest brother—as a quiet, peaceful man. On Sunday afternoons, when family members gathered on my grandmother's front porch, Paul settled in a chair at the far end of the porch, a tobacco pipe in his mouth. My father and other uncles smoked cigarettes and talked energetically about politics. But Paul sat and listened, chuckling lightly at something said or occasionally responding in his low voice.

He was a lean, long-limbed man, nearly six feet tall, and he had an East Tennessee accent brought from his birthplace Newcomb, Tennessee, a coal-mining community where my father's family lived before they moved to Western North Carolina.

During my childhood in the 1960s, Paul drove a taxicab for Eagle Cab Company in my hometown, Marion, North Carolina. On Saturday mornings my mother and I went downtown to shop, eat lunch, and mingle with the other folks who came into town that day. Since my mother didn't drive a car and my father sometimes worked on Saturday mornings at the hosiery mill or slept late, my mother called a cab to come get us and take us to town. A few minutes after my mother's telephone call, my uncle Paul would often be the cab driver who pulled up in front of our house in his white sedan. My mother and I hurried to the car and crawled into the back seat.

Once inside, I immediately sensed the warmth of the car's interior and the aroma of Paul's pipe smoke. While we drove up the highway, heading to town, I watched Paul's hands holding the steering wheel, his right hand shifting to support his pipe bowl. His movements were slow and easy as if he were in no hurry. He didn't say much during the drive, but made friendly small talk along the way.

Paul wore a plaid short-sleeved shirt, similar to those my father wore, and I noticed that one of Paul's arms was shorter than the other. Privately, my mother explained to me why Paul's arms looked unusual.

During World War II, while my father served in the Merchant Marines, my mother lived with his family. One day an official came to my grandmother's front door with news that Paul, who served in the Army, had been injured while fighting in North Africa, his shoulder severely wounded by shrapnel.

"She had five sons in the war at the same time," my mother reflected about my grandmother's sacrifice. "Five stars on her window."

Paul was returned to the United States and treated at a VA hospital near Asheville. My mother and my father's younger brother Glenn caught a bus and traveled thirty miles to see him.

"He was hurt bad," she said. She also noted that there were many other veterans at the VA hospital that day.

She recalled that when Paul came home from the hospital to recuperate, he had to lie in bed with his arm propped on a pillow.

While I rode in Paul's cab, I couldn't have imagined that two decades earlier he had experienced such a trauma. And in time I would learn more about Paul's past and how he had changed.

As a young man, Paul had been a hard drinker and a tempestuous lover, who lived like a hobo, jumping trains and drifting. But sometime after the war, he repented, found salvation through his Baptist faith, and gave up his dissolute behavior. He became a dedicated church member and settled into marriage at forty-five years old.

During preaching service on Sunday mornings at our family's church, the minister often asked, "Brother Paul, would you lead us in prayer?" Everyone grew still, awaiting Paul's words.

In Paul's prayer, he offered thanks for the Lord's mercy and for His blessings. And he invoked, "Dear Heavenly Father, we ask Thee to watch over our boys in foreign fields."

At the time, the Vietnam War was raging, and our community had suffered its losses. Though I didn't realize it then, Paul must have empathized with the soldiers, as did other veterans in the congregation. And mothers, like my own, feared for the safety of their sons who served in the military.

While Paul prayed, many were moved by the Spirit to utter, "Help us, Lord" and "Thank you, Lord." Some raised a hand in supplication.

Paul ended his lengthy prayer with a resounding *Amen*.

As the years passed, I saw Paul less and less. My grandmother died, ending the family gatherings. And eventually, my husband and I joined an Episcopal church, so I didn't hear Paul's prayers anymore.

One day I found myself driving behind Paul's white car, which had long been retired as a cab. While we were stopped at a red light, I looked through his rear window. Suddenly I perceived how much he resembled my father. And like my father, he had grown old.

The last time I saw Paul was a day in May 1991. I had gone home to visit my parents, and when I went into the house, I found my father in the front room, sitting alone on the couch.

"Where's Mother?" I asked. She had promised to make hamburgers for our lunch, but I didn't smell hamburger meat frying or hear sounds coming from the kitchen.

He told me my mother and my brother Butch had gone to the hospital.

"They say Paul had another stroke," he said, his voice tight with emotion.

"He's in bad shape."

We sat quiet for a while, and then he said, "He's my last brother."

"I know," I said, sadly acknowledging that his other four brothers had already died. After a minute, I stood from my chair and said, "I'm going to the hospital." I knew he didn't want to go, so I headed there myself, afraid of what I would find when I arrived. I'm sure my father had feared that, too.

At the hospital, my mother and brother stood in the hallway outside Paul's room. Paul's wife sat in a nearby waiting room, apparently in some consultation about removing Paul's life support.

With his wife's permission, I stepped into Paul's room.

He lay comatose in the hospital bed, his frail form covered by a white sheet. As I stood inside the door and watched the ventilator make his chest rise and fall, tears welled up in my eyes. How long had it been since I had spoken to him? How many words had we actually shared through the years? Very few, I admitted. Yet I felt close to him now and deeply sorry that I would lose him soon. Was it only now that I could fully appreciate how he, along with all those lost family members from my childhood, was important to me?

I said a silent prayer for Paul and quietly slipped out of his room, hoping in his way he knew that I had been there.

Later that day, Paul departed this life at seventy-seven years old.

He's gone now, but I remember him well by stories I have heard and by what I observed: he was a World War II Army hero who overcame a terrible injury; a dedicated Christian who held strong to his faith; and a dear uncle, whose calm presence was a comfort long ago and continues to be now as I remember him.

My Father's Pocket Knives

My father always carried a knife in his pants pocket.

During my childhood, I liked to watch him sharpen the clip blade of his pocket knife. He applied a thin layer of honing oil to his whetstone, and as he held the blade at an angle, he carefully stroked it across the stone till he was satisfied with the blade's edge. Then he wiped it clean with his handkerchief.

With his knife he would whittle me a wooden whistle or cut a piece of twine for the kite he'd made. He peeled me an apple with his pocket knife. In adulthood, I realized he contemplated a darker use for his knife. On a dreary September evening in 1989, my parents and I were on a return trip from Knoxville, Tennessee, where we had briefly visited my father's cousin Clyde and his family. I had driven us there earlier in the day, but with Hurricane Hugo threatening torrential rain and dangerous winds, I decided we'd better hurry back home to Marion, North Carolina.

As we neared an interstate rest area, my father said he wanted to stop. I asked, "Can you wait till we get home? It's not that much farther."

"No," he grumbled.

"Maybe we can find a McDonald's and use the restrooms there," I suggested, wary of interstate rest areas.

"No, I want to stop here," he said, and so we pulled onto the entrance ramp of the rest area. Only one other car was parked in the visitors' lot, and a grungy young man was walking up the sidewalk to the restroom building. I felt uneasy, especially for my father, who was seventy-one at the time and would have to be alone in the men's restroom with the stranger.

"Hurry and get back to the car," I urged him.

When my mother and I had returned to the car, we watched my father heading back down the sidewalk. I noticed he had his hand deep in his pants pocket.

After he settled in the front passenger seat, I told him to lock his door. "I was worried about you being in the restroom with that man," I said.

"I had this," he said and pulled out his little Case pocket knife. His remark made me sad, knowing he, too, had been anxious. There was a time when nothing seemed to scare him. I wondered if a pocket knife could have really protected him.

Yet I would come to understand that he was keenly aware of a pocket knife's capability as a weapon. One day he and I were searching for a document in his dresser drawer when I found a large black KA-BAR pocket knife.

"That was the knife my uncle Charlie stabbed me with," he said. His blunt statement surprised me. I was vaguely aware of a stabbing, but the incident had never been openly discussed in our family. I asked my mother about it, and she explained that it happened after my father returned home from World War II. One night, he, two of his brothers, his uncle Charlie, and another man were playing poker at her kitchen table. Suddenly, in a whiskey-fueled rage, Charlie stabbed my father in the hip and seriously injured him. I thought it odd that he had kept the knife that wounded him.

Through the years I occasionally bought my father a pocket knife for Christmas. He was always pleased with his new knife and began using it immediately. But he didn't throw away his old one; instead he stored it with others in his dresser drawer.

After my father passed away in 2006, my brothers and I divided his pocket knives. Along with a Case whittler and a Boker peanut knife, I asked for the KA-BAR stockman knife that had once belonged to his uncle Charlie. I guess some would question why I, like my father, would want to keep it.

I wonder if men today carry pocket knives like men of my father's generation did. Or have such knives gone the way of fedoras that you don't see men wear much anymore?

I know I will always treasure my father's pocket knives and can understand why he was reluctant to let any of them go.

The Family Rose

My mother says I inherited my affection for roses from my grandmother.

"Mama loved her roses," my mother tells me. "She had what she called 'monthly roses,' low rosebushes growing all along the edge of her yard, and I would buy her one every year for her birthday. Everybody in the family would get her a rosebush. Nobody loved flowers more than she did."

My grandmother's birthday fell on the same day as mine—April 16—and my husband and daughter now buy me rosebushes annually for my birthday.

Currently, I maintain two fenced rectangular rose gardens. One garden is located in front of my house, below my kitchen window, and is filled with hybrid teas, such as the patent roses *Mister Lincoln, Tahitian Sunset, Peace,* and *Oregold.* Reds, pinks, oranges, and yellows grace this garden. In another garden at the side of my house I have planted grandifloras and floribundas. But in this garden I have also planted a special shrub rosebush.

For years, I had heard stories about a "family rose" that had been passed down for generations through my mother's maternal line. This rosebush bloomed only in May and was said to have been brought from the "old country," though the particular country of origin remains vague. Like an Appalachian ballad, the legend of this rosebush is shrouded in mystery, but its authenticity is undeniable.

Years ago, on a spring day during an Easter break from my teaching job, I drove my mother to visit her older cousin Nancy, who had called her on the telephone and invited her to come see her rosebushes—descendants of the mythic family rose.

"I'll get you a cutting while you're here," Nancy promised.

Nancy lived in Old Fort—a township located at the western end of our county—on a rural road. Her older frame home was bordered by a tangle of large, unpruned shrub rosebushes.

I had brought a plastic pot filled with moist soil for my mother's cutting, and Nancy selected a bush and slit a couple of branches at the plant's base. I placed these cuttings in the pot, patting the soil to secure them.

After a visit on Nancy's front porch, we took the pot to my mother's house and set it on a picnic table in her backyard, where it would get plenty of sunlight. Soon one of the cuttings took root, and we transplanted it into her side yard, where it thrived and became a hardy rosebush with many leafy stems and abundant blooms.

In time, I decided I wanted to start a second rose garden at my home. And I knew which rosebush would be planted there first. I told my mother, "I want a cutting from the family rosebush."

"You ought to get one started," she agreed.

On a spring day I inspected her rosebush and felt hesitant to cut any of the branches. At the base I noticed a prickly cane—a sucker—that appeared to be independent from the plant. With a gloved hand, I pulled it up, being careful not to break its delicate roots. I placed it in a pot of enriched potting soil, watered it, and took it home to a sunny spot on my front porch.

After it took root in the pot, I moved it into my freshly prepared bed, intending to give it plenty of space when I added new rosebushes.

As typical of transplanted suckers, my antique rosebush showed no buds or blooms in its first season, but by the following May, it had grown several stems and produced a few blooms. Through the years it continued to thrive and grow taller and thicker, presenting more buds and blooms each season.

Today I keep the stalwart rosebush pruned to a neat width and height and stake it to keep it standing upright, as it tends to lean in the wind and rain. I lightly dust it upon the arrival of Japanese beetles—pests which would devour all its petals if I allowed—and I occasionally replenish the enriched soil at the bush's base to keep the roots healthy.

On that spring day, decades ago, when my mother's cousin Nancy gave her a cutting from her rosebush, she admonished, "Don't give a cutting to anybody outside of the family. This rosebush has always stayed in the family." Apparently this rule was part of the rosebush's myth.

Today, I tell my daughter, "I hope you'll take care of the rosebush after I'm gone." She knows it's an heirloom and part of our heritage. I explain the stipulation about exclusivity that seemed important to Nancy and likely to previous generations of rose gardeners in our family.

I will respect this obligation. Yet in May when I see the rosebush display its burgundy blossoms, so lovely and fragrant, I hope others notice it as they pass by my house. At least in this way I can share the family rose.

Boogerman

Growing up Southern Baptist, I was raised to believe in the power of both God and the Devil. Church sermons usually emphasized how easily anyone—including a child—could fall into the Devil's clutches. He was real and working to seize any soul weak or wicked enough to become his prey. A child might disobey his father or mother or he might steal something—these sins would make him vulnerable. A teenager might succumb to fleshly desires and commit fornication or, at least in my childhood Baptist church, drink an alcoholic beverage to be susceptible. And, of course, adults needed to be vigilant about honoring the Ten Commandments. Breaking any of these sacred rules put them at risk.

Being a Southern child, I had also heard about the boogerman. While in some places the word *boogerman* might be interpreted as a hobgoblin, to me, a Western North Carolinian, the word was always synonymous with the Devil. "If you don't quit doing that, the boogerman will get you" was a threat commonly used to adjust a child's behavior.

My idea of the boogerman was the cartoon (and Pagan) version: a red male creature that sported horns, a tail, and a goatee. He carried a pitchfork. In fact, I was even scared of pitchforks when I was a child. One summer day, some neighborhood kids and I were exploring an elderly neighbor's property. A rusted pitchfork hung on the side of his toolshed. When we saw this farm implement, we all took off running, thinking the Devil might be hiding in there. Maybe we thought the farmer was the Devil.

I first heard the name *Boogerman Johnson* when I was a child, listening to my mother's stories about growing up in the Clinchfield Manufacturing Company mill village. Her adventures in the cotton mill village, it seemed to me then, were as fascinating and exciting as those of Tom Sawyer. Recently, she once again talked about the house where she lived and its lack of indoor plumbing.

"We shared an outside toilet with the family next door," she said. "They were the Prices."

"What was your outhouse like?" I asked. I vaguely remembered the outhouse that stood in our own backyard when I was very young. In the late 1950s and early 1960s, many outhouses remained in our neighborhood. My father often credited President Franklin Delano Roosevelt for having such rural outhouses built as part of his WPA program. Our outhouse, as I recall, was a lumber building with a sloping tin roof. Inside was a wooden bench with a single hole cut in the center for the toilet seat. A hinged wooden lid covered the hole when the toilet wasn't in use. Our outhouse and others that I remember from that time usually held the lingering odor of human waste.

My mother described her own outhouse in the mill village.

"Well, it was a wooden building with two sections to it," she said and explained that it had two entrance doors and a privacy wall between the sections, so that her family and the family next door had an individual facility. "Our toilet hole was oblong," she added. She also noted with relief that the door could be secured from the inside to prevent accidental intrusions. Being modest, she said she hated to go to the outhouse if someone was in the other section.

Her daddy sometimes brought home rolls of toilet paper—a luxury—from the mill where he worked as an overseer in the card room. But otherwise the family made use of pages from the *Sears, Roebuck Catalogue*.

"We were afraid of spiders being down inside the toilet hole," she said. "You'd see webs in there. We'd heard about a young'un on the street being bit by a spider in the toilet."

And she explained that her older sister Ruby—a consummate housekeeper even as a girl—regularly cleaned the toilet.

"Sometimes in warm weather we took baths in the outside toilet," she said. "There was room to put a galvanized tub in there. After somebody took a bath, Ruby would use the old bathwater to scrub the toilet." According to my mother, Ruby washed around and inside the toilet seat to make sure it was free of spiders. "She kept the toilet fresh, and I don't remember it having a smell." She also noted, "We put kerosene inside the hole to kill infection, I reckon, and insects that might get in there. Thank goodness, nobody in the family smoked at that time."

But occasionally the toilet pits would fill up with fresh and decaying human waste. This is where Boogerman Johnson always entered my mother's story.

"Boogerman Johnson would come when the toilets got full and had to be cleaned out," she said. "He might have dug a new hole—I don't remember," she said.

My own investigation about outhouse cleaning techniques leads me to believe he probably removed the toilet bench and used a post-hole digger to remove the contents from the earthen pit, which was typically three to six feet deep. He might have brought along his wheelbarrow to deposit the waste in. Perhaps he then buried the waste.

Whatever technique he used to accomplish his task, Boogerman Johnson was the official toilet pit cleaner in the neighborhood where my mother lived, and he has figured prominently in her memories through the years.

When I was a child and my mother spoke of Boogerman Johnson, I immediately envisioned a sinister character.

I once asked her, "Do you know how Boogerman Johnson got his nickname?"

"I don't know why they called him 'Boogerman' Johnson. Children might have been scared of him because he cleaned out toilets."

It seemed possible to me that children gave him the nickname. Maybe they considered him spooky because of the repugnant materials he handled.

"Did he look scary?" I asked, still puzzled.

"Well," she said, "he was a little old guy with overalls and a bill cap. He probably was young, but he seemed old to me."

My mother would have been nine or ten years old at the time of this memory, based on the mill house in which her family lived during this era—"the upper house" as she called it, as opposed to another house at the foot of the hill where her family had lived in her earlier childhood.

According to my subsequent research on Johnson, who was born in 1884, he would have been around forty-eight years old when my mother knew him—hardly old, but to a child, the overalls and cap likely aged him.

In time I would come to learn more about this man whose nickname had mystified me since childhood.

My uncle John Ray, my mother's youngest brother, told me, "He lived up the street from our family. He had a pretty wife." How peculiar, I thought, that someone called *Boogerman* would have a pretty wife. I would later learn that after his first wife died, he soon remarried a much younger woman. She may have been the "pretty wife" my uncle remembered from his boyhood.

But the most stunning revelation about this man came during a casual conversation with my husband. We were talking one day about our family members and our cotton mill roots. In passing he said something about his great-grandfather Jeff Johnson who people called *Boogerman.*

Had I heard him right?

"Boogerman Johnson was your great-grandfather?" I asked. "The man who cleaned out toilets in Clinchfield?"

He laughed. "I reckon so," he said.

Years before this enlightening conversation with my husband, my aunt Carcenia, my father's older sister, had told me she knew the Johnson family. She said my husband's great-aunt Pearl was her best friend when they were girls, and Pearl's father, Jeff Johnson, was "one of the finest home builders in the county." My husband's grandmother Freda, Pearl's sister, had also proudly informed me that her father built a couple of houses in the neighborhood where I grew up. I'm sure these were houses I visited often as a child.

Thus I had some familiarity with Jeff Johnson, the house builder, through Carcenia and Freda's comments. But he had other skills, as well. My husband recently related that his great-grandfather was a trader of farm animals. And, indeed, Jeff Johnson's death certificate, dated 1951, lists his occupation as "cattle dealer."

Like my mother, my husband doesn't know why Jeff Johnson was nicknamed *Boogerman*. A few days ago, I asked my husband if he had any photographs of his great-grandfather. Searching through an old family album, he found a picture likely made around 1935, the same era in which my mother recalled Johnson. In the family portrait Johnson stands behind his seated children and grandchildren. He wears a dark dress coat, white shirt, and a black fedora that sits slightly back on his head. His hair is dark with some gray showing above his ears. A rawboned man, he has a long, angular face and a prominent nose. His close-set eyes stare intently at the photographer, and his eyebrows are knitted as if the sunlight bothers him. His lips are pressed together and turned downward, giving him a tired look. Although he is a strong patriarchal presence in the portrait, he is not a threatening one. His left hand rests protectively on his daughter Freda's shoulder, and all the children in his guardianship smile at the camera.

His face is now recorded in my memory—like so many others I have studied in family photographs—and I feel like I know him better for having seen his face.

And yet I am still puzzled.

My husband's father, who appears in the picture as a small boy sitting beside his mother, Freda, might have known why his grandfather was called *Boogerman*. But I didn't think to ask him while he was still alive. Now it's too late.

I've concluded that Jeff Johnson was a hard worker—a regular "Jack of all trades." Like so many others during the Great Depression and in the years afterward, he took whatever jobs he could find to support his family. He was a good man with an unlikely nickname that I will never understand.

A Real Farmer

During the Great Depression, my mother's daddy, Hosten Davis, was an overseer in the card room at Clinchfield Manufacturing Company in McDowell County, and his family lived in the cotton mill village.

The meager wages that my grandfather earned at the mill could scarcely cover expenses for his large family. So my grandmother Hessie, who would bear eleven children and whose grandchildren would call her *Mama Davis*, turned to her own resources to supplement her husband's income. These resources included raising a vegetable garden and keeping livestock.

After hiring a man to come with his horse and plow to prepare her garden plot, Mama Davis hoed the rows and planted seeds she'd ordered from *Spiegel Catalogue*. She used cow and chicken manure as fertilizer. Her oldest son, Herbert, and some of her other children sometimes helped her with the garden, but mostly she did the work herself. Growing up as a country girl, laboring in the fields, she had always been accustomed to hard work. In her mill village garden she raised corn, green beans, potatoes, onions, cabbage, and collard greens—"just about everything you'd plant," my mother says. My mother has often commented on her mama's Mr. Stripey tomatoes, saying they were "the prettiest big tomatoes," a slice filling a dinner plate.

My mother recalls a near-disaster in her mama's cornfield.

"One day a strong wind, like a tornado, blew down a part of her corn, laying the rows down flat. Mama went out and straightened up every bit of the corn. She wasn't going to let any of it go to waste."

When the garden's harvest came in, she used much of it for the family's meals, cooking the fresh vegetables and putting some up for later.

"She'd can green beans and kraut from cabbages and other vegetables in Mason jars," my mother says. "She kept them on shelves in the basement for us to eat throughout the year."

But she also sold some of her green beans to the mill's company store.

My mother remembers how she and one of her older sisters, Ruby or Helen, picked green beans in a tin tub and carried the tub to the store.

"We'd get a dollar for a tubful," she recalls; "it was more than a bushel."

Another resource that Mama Davis utilized was her milk cow, which she kept in a backyard pasture, a barn for its shelter. A milk cow was a common commodity in mill families, one encouraged by the mill owners. Mama Davis owned different cows through the years, but her last cow, Muley, was more like a pet. She owned this cow after my grandfather died and the family moved from the mill village to a nearby neighborhood. When Mama Davis died, Muley started bellowing miserably. My uncle Herbert tried to milk her, but "she wouldn't give a drop," my mother recalls. "It was sad, like she was grieving." Mama Davis had always been the one to milk Muley, and she wouldn't accept anyone else's attempts. The family was forced to sell her.

Through the years in the mill village, a cow provided ample sweet milk for the family to drink, but Mama Davis churned a portion to make buttermilk and butter, which she molded in a butter press. She sold some of this buttermilk and butter to neighbors in the village.

My grandmother also raised chickens.

"She had lots of chickens," my mother recalls. Oddly, her rooster was named *Henrietta,* and the chickens followed Mama Davis around like children.

"She raised the chickens from babies," my mother reflects, "and put the dibs (baby chicks) behind the kitchen woodstove in a box so they wouldn't get cold and die." She kept the chicks in this box until they were old enough to survive outside. Of course, some of the chickens provided meat for the table, especially on Sundays when the preacher came for dinner, and they also supplied eggs.

"She sold part of the brown eggs to neighbors," my mother explains. "The rest she stored in a drawer in a kitchen cabinet for the family to eat."

My grandmother was clearly industrious and, according to my mother, "liked to make a little money." Though Mama Davis lived and raised her family in a mill village near town, "she was a real farmer," my mother says. Her agricultural skills no doubt came from being raised on a country farm. Self-reliance was in her blood.

Sadly, I didn't know Mama Davis for long, as she died when I was six years old. Yet from my distant memories, my mother's recollections, and the family photographs I've seen, I feel I've known my grandmother well. It's from her, my mother says, that I inherited my green thumb and love of animals. Today when I work in my roses or plant my vegetable garden, I think about Mama Davis and hope I can live up to the legacy she has left me.

Her Clinchfield Childhood

As a child growing up in Clinchfield Manufacturing Company's cotton mill village in the twenties and thirties, my mother did not think of her family as poor. Indeed she might have felt privileged in contrast to her cousins who remained on family land in the country. They had no electricity, and their toilet was the woods. Yet she didn't consider her cousins poor, either, no more than they thought of themselves that way, and she enjoyed visiting them.

In the early days of my mother's childhood, during the Great Depression, there was much discussion of the plight of the cotton mill workers in our town. This discussion became national with the likes of folksinger Woody Guthrie performing a song "The Marion Massacre," lamenting the killing of strikers at Marion Manufacturing Company, and journalist Sinclair Lewis visiting our town and decrying the conditions of the mill families in newspaper articles that were later published in the pamphlet *Cheap and Contented Labor*. The Marion Textile Strike of 1929, which these famous voices responded to, was an event my mother remembers.

Not quite seven at the time, she saw National Guard troops who had come to guard the areas of East Marion and Clinchfield during the strike. Some gathered on the Clinchfield School grounds, their rifles braced at their sides. She and her friends sat on nearby railroad tracks and watched these guardsmen, thinking they were soldiers. From inside her house, she could look out the window and see strikers march by, holding their signs. At the time, her daddy, Hosten, worked as an overseer in the card room.

"Daddy didn't join the strike," she explained when I asked about the notorious event. "If he missed one week of work, we'd starve, so he continued to work."

In light of Sinclair Lewis' proclamation in his articles that the mill workers were underpaid and their families' living conditions deplorable, I asked my mother if she ever heard her daddy or mama complain about their life in the mill village.

"I never heard nobody complain," she said. "That was home." Thinking for a moment, she opened up.

"I don't remember them ever doing it. No, they didn't. They took it and didn't complain about it. That's the way we lived. They accepted it. Daddy was such a quiet man; he didn't do a lot of talking. He worked all the time. Nothing was ever said.

"We was just living a life that way, like everyone else lived. Older people would talk about politics sometimes. But they talked about everything. We was children—we accepted what we had and enjoyed what we had. We didn't know any different. We made our own fun. I got to go to the movies and to town."

My mother has often talked about her love of the movies and how much she enjoyed walking from the mill village, on the sidewalk that ran beside the highway, to town, over a mile away. Her main destination was the Marion Theatre. Opened in July 1929, the same month that saw an escalation of tension between mill management and workers, the Marion Theatre was a stately brick and carved stone structure with an imposing marquee. It must have seemed grand to the small town populace.

"Marion was crowded at that time," my mother explained; "everybody went to the movies. A line would be up the sidewalk—mostly younger people, but older people went, too. Different ages."

This remark made me think of the movie theater of my childhood and teenage years: the House Theatre. Built in the Art Deco style, this theater was opened in 1950 by the same family that had brought the Marion Theatre to town two decades earlier. Throughout my youth, I spent Friday or Saturday evenings sitting beside my mother in the dark auditorium, watching Disney films such as *Pinocchio* and *Cinderella* and later with girlfriends or a boyfriend, watching *Romeo and Juliet, Wuthering Heights,* and the vintage film *Gone With the Wind,* brought back for a new generation of viewers as well as for the earlier generation that had seen it thirty years before. Like the patrons of the Marion Theatre in my mother's childhood, we eager moviegoers of the 1960s and early 1970s stood in a line at the House Theatre to reach the ticket booth.

I asked my mother, "When did you usually go to the movies?" I knew we had always gone primarily on weekend nights. She laughed and said, "Morning, noon, and night. I was a movie freak."

She admitted that sometimes she "skipped school" to go to the movies on a weekday. To avoid passing the school on her way to town and risk being caught, she said she had to "go back of the mill" and walk through a section of Clinchfield known as "the New Hill." She took this route, she said, "so no one would see me."

"How much did the movie ticket cost?" I asked her, realizing money was tight then.

"It cost five cents to go to the movies till you were about eleven years old and then a dime," she said.

She explained that sometimes in front of the theater stood life-sized wax figures of popular movie actors, such as Clark Gable and Bob Steele. They were dressed in costumes from the movies, she said, and looked so real that it seemed like the actual stars were there.

"What were some popular movies at that time?" I asked.

She noted *Wagon Wheels* with Randolph Scott and *Our Gang* comedies.

She also mentioned the films of Fred Astaire and Ginger Rogers and of course Shirley Temple.

At her home in Clinchfield, she imitated these tap dancing stars. She had studied their moves on the screen and practiced them on her house's wooden floorboards. Her mama, Hessie, had fitted her shoes with metal plates, so her taps could be heard throughout the house.

She also "put on shows" like the *Our Gang* kids did. In her daddy's barn, located behind the Methodist church, she and other children from the village danced, sang, and acted, charging neighbors a penny or a safety pin for admission. Sometimes parents would come to see their children perform.

"I was the producer and director," she said. I suspected she was also the star of these shows. Thinking about it now, I believe her aspirations to get to Hollywood and be a movie star might have instigated her years of coaching me for school talent shows as a singer of such standards as "Side By Side" and "Breezin' Along With the Breeze." She always accompanied me on the piano for these performances. Most of my schoolmates then had never heard these old songs before. At the age of four I sang "Bye Bye Blackbird" a cappella—my first public performance—for visiting family.

Besides going to the movies and putting on musical shows for the neighborhood, my mother also spent happy moments in the mill village at Christmastime.

"Daddy walked in the snow to hunt us a Christmas tree in some nearby woods," she said. "Seems like it snowed every Christmas back then. He found us a simple pine tree. Mama decorated it with little crepe paper bells and cotton balls. To us it was the most beautiful thing we'd ever seen. We hung our black stockings on the mantle."

On Christmas Eve, she walked through the snow to attend a Baptist church service. "The church was a wooden frame one," she said, "and I remember the Christmas tree in the church. Gifts hung from the limbs of the tree. My gift was a box of handkerchiefs."

"Did you get any toys for Christmas?" I asked, remembering treasures I found under our tinsel-covered tree on Christmas mornings: a Quick Draw McGraw doll, a Tru-Vue Projection Theatre, a Troll Village. . . .

"If I was lucky," she replied, "Mama bought me a doll in a peanut shell. You opened up the shell, and there was a doll inside. At the time, it cost a dollar, and a dollar was a lot of money." I've often heard her speak of the miniature baby doll in a peanut shell that her mama bought for her, apparently as dear a gift to her as any imaginable.

She said that on Christmas morning, children also looked forward to seeing horse-drawn wagons that carried "pokes" of treats to the mill houses. She noted that these horse-drawn wagons were used when she was "real little" but were eventually replaced by trucks. Every member of the mill family received a poke.

"What was in your Christmas poke?" I asked, recalling Christmas pokes from my childhood Baptist church. We would get our pokes after the Christmas play, as we exited the church's sanctuary.

"A lot of stuff," she said. "Apples, oranges, nuts, chewing gum, bananas, hard Christmas candy." These were the same contents I remembered from my own childhood Christmas pokes.

She added that her daddy stayed late at the mill on Christmas Eve to help fill pokes that would be delivered the next morning. "He'd bring home leftovers," she said, which meant extra Christmas treats for the family.

Christmas was a happy time for my mother and her family. But admittedly, life was harder then, though my mother has never emphasized this point. Everyday conveniences were rare, and I've asked her about common issues of comfort.

"What kind of heat did you use?" I asked.

"Coal in fireplaces," she said, "and wood in the kitchen woodstove. Mama always cooked on a woodstove. It helped heat the house, too."

"Where did you get the coal?"

"The coal yard near West Marion," she said. This coal yard still remained during my childhood in the 1960s, when people in my county still commonly used coal as a heat source.

She said they bought wood from a man named Mr. Shuford.

"What about bathroom facilities?" I asked.

"We had an outside toilet at the back of the house," she said. "There was a path to the toilet." This setup was typical of all the houses in the mill village, and my mother has noted that two families shared a privy, the structure having two toilet sections, a privacy wall in between, and separate entry doors.

I was not unaccustomed to such a toilet facility. In my childhood, most houses in our neighborhood had an outhouse in the backyard—built, according to my father, during Franklin Roosevelt's WPA program. The outhouses were soon abandoned as people acquired indoor plumbing and modern bathrooms. But I well remember these little lumber buildings with their hard bench and toilet hole and distinctive feculent smell.

"Did you go out at night when you had to go to the bathroom?"

"I always went out at night," she said. "I'd wake Mama to go out with me. Older people used slop jars."

"You mean like a chamber pot?" I asked.

"Older people kept one under their bed," she said. "We never used one except when Grandma came to visit." She has often mentioned her maternal grandma Ledford coming from the country to stay with her family.

She was quick to add that her daddy would sometimes bring home rolls of toilet paper from the mill, which was a luxury in contrast to *Sears, Roebuck Catalogue* pages that they typically used.

"What about baths?" I asked.

"We heated water on the woodstove and filled a big galvanized tub and took baths behind the woodstove. Nobody could see you back there. Sometimes we took a bath in the outside toilet, which was large enough for the tub." She explained that after the bath was over, the soapy water was used to scrub their toilet. Her older sister Ruby, a meticulous housekeeper, did the toilet scrubbing, washing the floor and the toilet seat inside and out.

"How did you wash your hair?" I asked, aware of her phobia about getting a sore throat from a wet head. I also knew from her stories about her early life that she frequently suffered from sore throats, specifically a serious inflammation of the tonsils known as *quinsy*.

"When I was little," she had related, "I kept a sore throat all the time. Mama would doctor it every way she could. She'd even give me a laxative—BLACK-DRAUGHT—and a nickel to take it. I don't know why she gave me a laxative for a sore throat. But nothing helped, so she had to call Dr. Miller, the company doctor. He charged three dollars to come to the house." She noted that this fee was deducted from her daddy's pay.

The quinsy, she said, would make her tonsils swell so severely that the doctor would have to lance them to release the pus. Penicillin wasn't available then, so lancing was his primary treatment, though at one point he scheduled my mother for a tonsillectomy at his office in town. Having arrived at his office on the scheduled day, she panicked when she heard him rattling his surgical instruments and ran back home before he could operate. She never did get her tonsils removed.

In terms of washing her hair, she explained, "We never had running water. Mama had a well on the back porch, and we had to draw water out and bring it inside. We heated the water on the woodstove and washed our hair in a sink. We used soap for shampoo when I was little."

"How did you dry it?" I asked. I knew even in my childhood, I dried my hair at the blower on our Seigler oil heater that stood in our front room. We didn't own a hand-held blow dryer then.

"We stood on a chair under a light bulb," she said. "Mama didn't allow us to leave our hair wet." She went on to say that if she or her siblings came in at night with hair wet from rain, her mama made them dry their hair before going to bed. I believe her bouts with quinsy and her mama's wariness of wet heads caused my mother to guard my habits as a child and teenager. She forbade me to wash my hair when I had tonsillitis or strep throat or go outside or to bed with my head wet. I have enforced these same rules with my daughter.

In answering my questions, my mother never complained about the circumstances of her early life. She stated the conditions of her past existence in a matter-of-fact manner. Clearly, she had no more felt indignant at drying her hair under a hot light bulb than I resented drying mine on my knees at an oil heater. It's just how life was then.

I learned that the difficulties of my mother's childhood were overshadowed by the pleasures and beauty she experienced at that time. In our conversations, she recalled the two mill houses that her family lived in, relocating from one house to another on the same street when she was nine.

"Our first house was a four-room house," she said and added that the second house might have been slightly larger and was considered a "better house"—a kind of step up, she thought, because of her daddy's job promotion. Her friend Katie Mae and her family had lived in that house, but when Katie Mae's daddy "got a higher job," they moved into an even nicer home. So, my mother said, "we got to move into their house." When she was little, she had often visited Katie Mae in this house, and she liked the way it smelled of apples, from the sacks of apples stored in their closet.

Regardless of which mill house my mother's family lived in, she emphasized that her mama "always had a nice living room. She might have had a lot of children," my mother said, "but the living room was always clean."

Indeed her mama would ultimately bear eleven children, though one son, my mother's younger brother Earl, died of colitis when he was a baby, not quite fifteen months old. My mother often remarks how pretty Earl was, with his blond hair and blue eyes. She remembers how sick he became with diarrhea and how she cried when he died. Though she was only five at the time, she remembers his death vividly and still grieves it. Her only existing photograph of Earl is one of him in his casket—a common photographic custom in those days.

Through the years, my mother has often spoken of their stylish living room, which she credits to her mama, and of a beautiful table lamp with a bead-fringed shade that graced this room. She has lamented that her mama eventually gave the lamp away to a relative in the country and wishes she herself had gotten it. Besides the lamp, she has also noted other decor in their living room: an upright piano, a long rug, and a living room suite—everything her mama could afford to make an attractive, comfortable place for her family to gather in.

I asked her where her mama acquired these living room furnishings. She said her mama ordered items from a *Sears, Roebuck Catalogue* or *Spiegel Catalogue*, and she also purchased furniture from Smith Furniture Company, a local store. All of the purchases were "paid for on time," she said, and she noted that this was the only way her mama could have afforded them.

One of the central and most beloved features of the Davis living room was an Atwater Kent console radio that her family had for years.

"We usually listened to it at night," she said. She recalled *Lum and Abner* and *Fibber McGee and Molly* as radio shows that her whole family gathered to listen to. She added that on Saturday night, "everybody looked forward to the *Grand Ole Opry*." She said you could go outside and hear the program playing in other mill houses on the street. "It was on in everyone's house, seemed like."

But her daddy especially enjoyed listening to President Roosevelt's *Fireside Chats*.

A few years earlier, her family, joined by neighbors, had sat in their living room and sung World War I songs.

"I was just a little bitty thing," she said. "This was eight years after the war—I was four years old." I imagined the group, adults and children, sitting in lamplight singing "There's a Long, Long Trail" and "Till We Meet Again."

Happy times were experienced in their quaint living room that her mama took such pains to decorate. It was not a bleak room, nor their house desolate like those mill houses that Sinclair Lewis described in his writings.

Her mama also took pride in her yard—a dirt yard typical of the time and place—that my mother's oldest sister, Clarabel, regularly swept clean.

"Mama always had beautiful flowers," she said, "—roses and zinnias— in her yard and along the walk." In the photograph of my mother's brother Earl, who is dressed in a white burial gown and lies in a tiny casket lined with white cloth, he holds a rose in his left hand. The casket rests against the family's wooden front porch steps. My mother has explained that her mama cut this rose from her rosebush beside the front porch and placed it in Earl's hand.

My mother inherited her mama's love of flowers and ability to grow them. In my childhood yard my mother grew abundant beds of snapdragons, marigolds, tulips, and other varieties of colorful, fragrant flowers. I credit my own love of flowers to my mother and grandmother. Now while I work in my own two rose gardens, I especially think of my grandmother.

My grandmother's gardening skills were also exhibited in her vegetable gardening, which provided food for the family and extra income. One instance of an unexpected benefit from the garden was explained by my mother.

"Mama had a cornfield," she said. "I found a nickel in the cornfield, and I used that to go to my first movie—a silent movie—the first movie I'd ever seen in my life." She said that she walked to the theater that day with her older sister Helen.

Besides corn, my grandmother's garden bore a harvest of "cornfield beans," explained by my mother as green beans whose vines twined around the corn stalks.

"Either Helen and me or Ruby and me gathered green beans in a tin tub," my mother explained. "We picked it in a little bit and took it to the company store. They gave us a dollar for a tub of beans."

Her mama also canned green beans for the family, along with kraut from cabbages, and "about anything else" she raised, my mother said. These canned goods were kept on shelves in their basement and used for meals throughout the year.

"We picked blackberries along a path to the lake, mostly my sisters and me. Maybe Daddy would go along." She said her mama made cobblers and jelly out of the berries. I thought of my mother's past canned jars of strawberry preserves and how good the sweet preserves filled with tart strawberries tasted in a hot buttered biscuit. Our family quickly went through her many jars of strawberry preserves.

I knew my grandmother also raised livestock and asked my mother about the animals she had on her property in the mill village.

"She raised a hog. My uncle Manley or my uncle Lester took the hog to the country, Montford's Cove, where Grandma and all my people lived. They killed it and worked it up there. They had a smokehouse where they kept the meat. They got part of it, see?" She noted that her mama canned sausage from the dressed meat and made liver mush. She also said her mama made "meat skins," more commonly known as fried pork rinds. These, she said, "we loved."

"She kept a cow," my mother added. "Mama churned the milk and turned it into buttermilk and made butter in a press. One of the things I remember her doing is churning." Some of this buttermilk and butter was sold to neighbors in the village.

"Mama always had chickens. I never knew of her not to have chickens. She'd cook one of our chickens when the Baptist preacher came to eat with us on Sunday after church."

She explained that the younger children had to sit on the back step and wait for their meal while the preacher, her mama, daddy, and older siblings sat at the table and ate first. "Mama would give us an orange to eat while the older people was eating." She laughed and said if the children had gone to the table first, they would have eaten everything before the adults had a chance.

"We couldn't wait till they got gone from the table so we could eat," she said. "I always wanted the chicken breast. I was hoping they would leave some of the chicken breast in the chicken and dumplin's. If we was lucky, there was some left. That was a big day for us. Mama always made chocolate cake." In a quieter voice, she added, "That was one of my fondest memories—when we sat on the step eating oranges." I imagined that her anticipation of the fine meal was a great pleasure. "We didn't care to wait till they got through, hoping they'd leave the chicken breast." And she noted that there was always plenty of food to eat when the older people finally left the table.

"Besides chicken and dumplings and chocolate cake," I asked, "what did your mama prepare for these meals when the preacher came to dinner?"

"She'd fix creamed potatoes and vegetables she had."

"What did she serve to drink?" I asked. "Milk?"

"Tea or coffee."

"Where did your family eat? Was there a dining room?"

"We ate in the kitchen at a long table with a white table cloth. It was a big room."

I recalled my mother saying that if her daddy hadn't worked during the textile strike, her family would have starved. But I knew she was exaggerating then because of the meals her mama managed to create from her own industriousness.

"Was your mama a good cook?" I asked.

"Yes, she was a good cook!" my mother asserted, almost incredulous that I could ask such a question. She mischievously added, "Who do you think I got mine after?" She meant her cooking skills. I couldn't argue with her there, as I recalled her delicious meals, especially our Sunday dinners of pinto beans, steak and gravy, creamed potatoes, slaw, homemade biscuits, and strawberry cobbler. The dining room table was so crowded with dishes of food that there was hardly room for our plates.

My mother reflected, "Many a time I watched her cook and tried to help. When she'd mix up cake batter, we'd want to get that and eat it."

This recollection reminded me of my mother's chocolate and coconut cakes and the times when my brother Steve and I, as children, would stand and wait for my mother to finish spooning her creamy cake batter into the baking pans. She would give one of us the mixer beaters to lick and the other the bowl to scrape.

"What were some favorite foods she cooked?" I asked.

"Macaroni and cheese was my favorite dish," she answered quickly. Often she has reminisced about her mama's tasty macaroni and cheese, which she said was "soupy," meaning the cheese sauce was milky in consistency. This is exactly the way she herself prepared it through the years and the way I do now.

She recalled that her mama always wanted to feed anyone who was hungry.

"When my brothers came home from the Second World War," she said, "she'd get up, build a fire, and cook them breakfast. She did that many a time." She emphasized that her brothers would come in at different times, and her mama would cook each of them a separate breakfast.

Her mama also wouldn't let a hobo leave her house hungry. Apparently hoboes would jump off the train from nearby railroad tracks and approach houses to beg for food. My mother's older brother, Herbert, once told me that the hoboes knew the houses where food would be given.

"They'd come to the back door," my mother said, "and she fixed them cornbread and milk. Anything left over from our meal, she'd give them." My mother also noted how kindly her mama spoke to the hoboes, calling them "honey," a term of endearment that she used with everyone.

In my mother's stories of her Clinchfield childhood, which she still shares with me, she doesn't stress the poverty or deprivation that a journalist once perceived in the lives of the cotton mill workers and their families. Instead, she emphasizes the love and security of family and community that she felt and the virtues of industriousness and charity that she witnessed. She has always been proud that her daddy did not miss a day of work for thirty-some years until his death at fifty-two. And she does not blame his premature death of a cerebral hemorrhage on his cotton mill work.

"He didn't go to a doctor the way he should have," she explains. "People didn't go to the doctor back then like they do now. He never went to doctors. That's the reason. It wasn't his job."

By everything my mother has told me through the years, both her parents were hard-working people, raising a large family, and getting by the best they could. It's what people did during the Great Depression. Life for the mill families, such as my mother's family, the Davises, was a struggle to be sure, with times of difficulty and sadness. And the journalist who came to town and exposed the harsh conditions of the workers and their families likely had honorable intentions and revealed some truth.

Yet I believe this outsider didn't realize that the cotton mill families of Marion also experienced moments of joy, beauty, and pride that were as real to them as the hardships they faced along the way.

ACKNOWLEDGMENTS

I gratefully acknowledge the following magazines and literary journals that originally published my essays, sometimes in slightly different form or with different title:

Smoky Mountain Living: "Night Visitor," "Silo," "My Mother's Snow Cream," "My Christmas, 1967," "Our Garden Snake," "Hornets' Nest," and "My Father's Pocket Knives"

Cowboy Jamboree: "Laddie" and "House Next Door"

Self-Reliance: "The Fun We Made"

Southern Roots Magazine: "Desk and Chair"

WNC Magazine: "Saturdays at the Mill"

BoomerMagazine.com: "A Horse of My Own"

Connotation Press: "The Party" and "The Cherokee Sweethearts"

Blue Ridge Outdoors: "Copperheads"

Blue Ridge Country: "Watching Crows," "The Christmas Hawk," and "The Stone Cutter's Tools"

Backwoods Home Magazine: "Scarecrow"

Blue Ridge Motorcycling: "Those Golden Years"

Countryside: "The Family Rose"

Red Dirt Forum: "Her Clinchfield Childhood"

Julia Nunnally Duncan is author of eleven books of fiction, nonfiction, and poetry, including, among others, *Blue Ridge Shadows* (Iris Press), *Drops of the Night* (March Street Press), *A Place That Was Home* (eLectio Publishing), and *A Neighborhood Changes* (Finishing Line Press). As a freelance writer, she is a frequent contributor to *Smoky Mountain Living Magazine* and has published essays, stories, and poems in numerous other magazines and literary journals. Her hometown, Marion, North Carolina, her working-class childhood in the 1960s, and her family—present and past—permeate her writing.

Julia earned a B.A. in English and an M.F.A. in Creative Writing from Warren Wilson College, and she taught English and Southern Culture at McDowell Technical Community College for over thirty years.

She lives in a rural community near the Pisgah National Forest in Western NC with her husband, Steve, a woodcarver, and enjoys spending time with him and their daughter, Annie.

Milton Keynes UK
Ingram Content Group UK Ltd.
UKHW011103201123
432908UK00007B/1359